Mecklermedia's Official
Internet World™

60 Minute Guide to Java

Mecklermedia's Official
Internet World™

60 Minute Guide to Java

Ed Tittel

and

Mark Gaither

IDG Books Worldwide, Inc.
Foster City, CA • Chicago, IL • Indianapolis, IN • Braintree, MA • Dallas, TX

Mecklermedia's Official Internet World™
60 Minute Guide to Java™
Published by

IDG Books Worldwide, Inc.
An International Data Group Company
919 East Hillsdale Boulevard, Suite 400
Foster City, CA 94404

Library of Congress Catalog Card No.:
ISBN 1-56884-711-4
Printed in the United States of America
First Printing,October, 1995
10 9 8 7 6 5 4 3 2

Distributed in the United States by IDG Books Worldwide, Inc.

Published in the United States

For More Information...

For general information on IDG Books in the U.S., including information on discounts and premiums, contact IDG Books at 800-434-3422.

For information on where to purchase IDG's books outside the U.S., contact Christina Turner at 415-655-3022.

For information on translations, contact Marc Jeffrey Mikulich, Foreign Rights Manager, at IDG Books Worldwide; fax number: 415-655-3295.

For sales inquiries and special prices for bulk quantities, contact Tony Real at 800-434-3422 or 415-655-3048.

For information on using IDG's books in the classroom and ordering examination copies, contact Jim Kelly at 800-434-2086.

Internet World 60 Minute Guide to Java is distributed in Canada by Macmillan of Canada, a Division of Canada Publishing Corporation; by Computer and Technical Books in Miami, Florida, for South America and the Caribbean; by Longman Singapore in Singapore, Malaysia, Thailand, and Korea; by Toppan Co. Ltd. in Japan; by Asia Computerworld in Hong Kong; by Woodslane Pty. Ltd. in Australia and New Zealand; and by Transworld Publishers Ltd. in the U.K. and Europe.

From Internet World Books

With INTERNET WORLD books, the first name in Internet magazine publishing and the first name in Internet book publishing now join together to bring you an exciting new series of easy-to-use handbooks and guides written and edited by the finest Internet writers working today.

Building upon the success of *Internet World* magazine and in close cooperation with its staff of writers, researchers, and Net practitioners, INTERNET WORLD books offer a full panoply of Net-oriented resources—from beginner guides to volumes targeted to business professionals, Internet publishers, corporate network administrators, and web site developers, as well as to professional researchers, librarians, and home Internet users at all levels.

These books are written with care and intelligence, with accuracy and authority, by the foremost experts in their fields. In addition, the bundling of potent connectivity and search software with selected titles in the series will broaden their inherent usefulness and provide immediate access to the vast fluid contents of the Internet itself.

One key element illuminates all of these features—their focus on the needs of the reader. Each book in this series is user-friendly, in the great tradition of IDG Books, and each is intended to bring the reader toward proficiency and authority in using the Internet to its fullest as a complement to all the other ways the reader creates, gathers, processes, and distributes information.

The scope of INTERNET WORLD books is to serve you as Internet user, whether you are a dedicated "nethead" or a novice sitting down to your first session on the Net. Whatever your level, INTERNET WORLD books are designed to fulfill your need. Beyond this, the series will evolve to meet the demands of an increasingly literate and sophisticated Net audience, presenting new and dynamic ways of using the Internet within the context of our business and personal lives.

Alan M. Meckler
Chairman and C.E.O.
Mecklermedia Corporation

Christopher J. Williams
Group Publisher and V.P.
IDG Books Worldwide, Inc.

Credits

IDG Books Worldwide, Inc.

Group Publisher and V. P.
Christopher J. Williams

Publishing Director
John Osborn

Senior Acquisitions Manager
Amorette Pedersen

Managing Editor
Kim Field

Editorial Director
Anne Marie Walker

Production Director
Beth A. Roberts

Project Editor
Ralph E. Moore

Manuscript Editor
Jerry Olsen

Technical Editor
Steven Harrington

Composition and Layout
Benchmark Productions, Inc.

Proofreader
Joan Fitzgerald

Indexer
Liz Cunningham

Book Design
Benchmark Productions, Inc.

Cover Design
Draper and Liew Inc.

Mecklermedia Corporation

Senior Vice President
Tony Abbott

Managing Editor
Carol Davidson

Acknowledgments

Mark Gaither: Many thanks to the IDG folks, especially Ralph Moore for his patience and understanding. Thanks to Ed Tittel for believing in me one more time. A lot of thanks to three hard-working and gracious system engineers at Sun Microsystems in Austin and San Antonio: Brian Strandtman, Philip Helsel, and Gary Cassens. Thanks to Sid Conklin at Stanford University for the WebLogger code. Thanks to Paul Ambrose at WebLogic for his valuable input. Thanks to the souls on the Java and HotJava mailing lists who continually help to mold Java into a first-rate programming language. Last, thanks to my folks for their understanding: Norman and Linda at Tierra Linda Ranch, and my brothers Paul and Adam for their undying support.

Ed Tittel: I'd like to start by thanking my Mom, Ceceilia Katherine Kociolek Tittel, who fostered my appreciation of language from a young and tender age. I don't think I'd be writing these words if it weren't for you. Thanks, Mom! I'd also like to thank Mark Gaither, the man who shrinks from no new technology, no matter how wild and woolly! Let me add my thanks to my family for putting up with yet another crazy publication schedule when I was supposed to be taking a "rest." Suzy, Austin, and Chelsea: Thanks for dealing with me in my wounded-bear stage. To Dusty, my ever-faithful Labrador: You're the only one who sees it all, buddy! Thanks for sticking so close when the going got weird.

This book is very much a team effort, so the thanks don't stop here. Together, both of us would like to thank Michael Stewart of Impact On-Line for his work on this book, and for his many efforts on our behalf. We also have to thank the folks at Sun Microsystems who made Java and HotJava happen, and for all those who helped us and answered our sometimes inane and incongruous questions.

Finally, we'd like to thank the whole IDG production team—including Ralph Moore, our project editor, Steve Harrington, our crackerjack technical editor, and Jerry Olsen, our macho but magnificent manuscript editor—for all the help they gave in putting this book together. Last, but by no means least, we'd also like to thank our old friends and partners in grime, Anne Marie Walker and Amy Pedersen, for giving us yet another chance to work together.

The publisher would like to give special thanks to Patrick McGovern, without whom this book would not have been possible.

About the Authors

Mark Gaither is a software engineer at HaL Software Systems in Austin, TX. He's part of a five-person team that maintains and extends an SGML filtering gateway for HaL's wonderful tech writers. Mark's experience with SGML started by chance when he was volunteered to aid Steven DeRose, who delivered an introduction to SGML and hypertext at Hypertext '92. As a result, Mark's SGML experience has blossomed into the WWW world. He righteously evangelizes valid HTML and maintains HaL's HTML Validation Service and HTML Check Toolkit, available at: http://www.hal.com/~markg/WebTechs/.

Mark also religiously answers Dr. Web technical queries (at http://www.stars.com/Dr.Web/) from HTML and WWW neophytes worldwide. Mark is a co-founder and the current director of the Austin WWW Users Group, and is a member of the board of directors of the Austin Area Multimedia Alliance. Finally, Mark was graduated from Texas A&M University in 1990, with a B.S. in Computer Science. He is currently finishing his Masters of Computer Science at TAMU.

You may contact Mark at markg@aus.sig.net or markg@hal.com.

Ed Tittel likes to write PC-related books. He created IDG Books' best-selling *NetWare for Dummies* with Deni Connor and Earl Follis, and co-authored *HTML for Dummies* with Steve James. Most recently, Ed joined forces with Mark Gaither, Sebastian Hassinger, and Mike Erwin to write *Foundations of WWW Programming* for IDG Programmers Press Professional.

Ed teamed with Bob LeVitus to pen the best-selling *Stupid DOS Tricks*, *Stupid Windows Tricks*, and *Stupid Beyond Belief DOS Tricks*. With Robert Wiggins, Ed co-authored *The Trail Guide to CompuServe*. With Margaret Robbins, Ed wrote three *...Essentials* books on network design, e-mail, and the Internet.

In a past life, Ed was director of technical marketing at Novell, where he worked for six years. Ed contributes regularly to the computer trade press, with an emphasis on networking technology. His credits include *Infoworld*, *LAN Times*, *LAN Magazine*, *Iway*, *MacWEEK*, *MacWorld*, *Maximize*, *NetGuide*, and *Computer Shopper*.

You may contact Ed at etittel@zilker.net.

Contents

Contents

*Intro***duction**

elcome to the bleeding edge of computer language technology! As we write this book, the programming language known as Java remains very much a moving target. Although the specifications are more or less complete, we found ourselves dealing with alpha release code and an incomplete programming environment in researching and writing this book. We also stumbled into more than a few holes in current tools and implementations as we groped our way toward the book's conclusion.

By the time you read this, things should have settled down quite a bit. That will help to reduce the sources of uncertainty about Java, as will more widespread design and development experience in Java. We can only hope that by alerting you to our own mistakes and steering you around the hazards we encountered, our experiences can be your guide and help you master this fascinating environment quickly and easily.

About this Book

There are two fundamental ways to think of this book:
1. It is built to be approached as a series of three, 60 minute tutorials on Java, with each tutorial delivering a specific lesson or set of information on the subject.

2. It is meant to be an overview of the current state of Java arts, but also to provide signposts to more current information, since Java is itself a moving target right now.

In neither case is this book meant to be an exhaustive reference work on Java. Rather, it should serve you as an introduction to the language's concepts and capabilities, and provide an entry point to the collection of information about, tools for, and examples of Java available on the Internet.

What is Java?

Java is both a programming environment and a language produced by Sun Microsystems, Inc. It's yet another of the new breed of object-oriented languages and has been designed to solve problems in the area of client-server programming.

Java was created as part of a large project at Sun whose mission was to develop complex and advanced software applications intended for small electronic devices. These devices are portable, distributed, reliable, and real-time embedded systems aimed at general consumers. Earlier attempts at such devices have had such names as Digital Assistants or Portable Data Assistants (PDAs).

Sun's first attempt at these software applications was intended to be implemented in C++. But because of nasty compiler snafus and a growing list of problems with C++—mainly memory leaks and multiple inheritance problems—Sun ditched C++ and implemented a new language, Java. Since its inception in 1992, many other applications for Java have surfaced. For this book, we find Java's ability to create applets that can be embedded in HTML documents especially interesting.

The Java architecture is neither radical nor especially new. In a nutshell, Java applications are compiled into an architecture-neutral bytecode. This bytecode can then be executed on any platform that supports a Java interpreter. Java requires only one source and one binary, yet can run on many platforms, making it a maintainer's dream. Figure Intro-1 depicts the Java architecture and its system requirements.

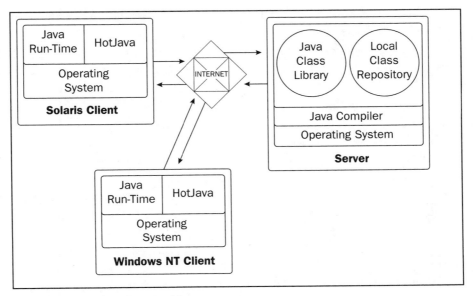

Figure Intro-1: The Java architecture

The following quote is from the Sun Microsystems first white paper on Java:

Java: A simple, object-oriented, distributed, interpreted, robust, secure, architecture-neutral, portable, high-performance, multi-threaded, and dynamic language.

Whew! That's quite a string of buzzwords. These are the main characteristics of Java, describing both the Java programming language and its runtime environment.

Sun has also created a new WWW browser called HotJava. HotJava utilizes most of the browsing techniques found in other popular WWW browsers such as Mosaic and Netscape. The main difference between HotJava and other browsers is HotJava's ability to add new behavior to an HTML document (which can only be viewed with HotJava). All other WWW browsers are tightly bound to the supported protocols and data formats. These other browsers won't be able to take advantage of this added behavior; but with HotJava, static documents can come alive.

In typical WWW browsers, rendered data is limited to text, low-quality audio and video, and images. With HotJava, the types of data that can be rendered are endless. You can add functionality to the browser by extending the protocols and data types it can handle on the fly, including new document types and delivery mechanisms.

HotJava also provides a seamless and transparent access method to such applications. These applications are simply passed along the network from the server to your HotJava browser. If the browser doesn't recognize the data format, it goes back to the server to get the specialized application required to view the new format. You no longer need to install such applications at your site as you currently must for helper applications for other WWW browsers. With Java and HotJava, the necessary application just arrives, ready to run!

The beauty of this concept is that if you develop an application for the Web, you need not be concerned if this application is installed at a user's site. With Java and HotJava, it arrives where it's needed. This transparent retrieval of specialized applications lets developers break out of a limited set of data types, and allows them to develop and deliver any type of software application imaginable via the Web.

Other characteristics of the HotJava browser include interactive content, dynamic data types, and dynamic protocols.

- **Interactive content** describes Java's ability to add content interactively and dynamically. For example, a software developer could write a Java application that deploys a hotrod engine rebuilding simulation. Hotrodders using HotJava on the Web could load this simulation and interact with it through an input device such as a mouse, a microphone, or a joystick.

- **Dynamic data types** allow HotJava to dynamically link a specialized Java application to a referenced server that supports new data types. The Java application can dynamically add behavior to HotJava and allow the browser to render that data.

- **Dynamic protocols** allow seamless integration of new protocols with existing ones. This should have a profound effect on the way business is conducted on the Internet in the future. No longer will specialized clients and servers be required to support particular functionality, such as electronic commerce.

As you might expect, HotJava is written in Java. Because it's a fully-functional, stand-alone program, HotJava is a Java application. On the other hand, a Java applet is a compiled Java program that is included within an HTML document using the <APP> tag.

In this book, you learn how to write both Java applets and Java stand-alone applications. You also learn how to take advantage of Java's dynamic, extensible nature to add new capabilities to HTML documents and browsers, and how to create new Java applications from existing code and class libraries.

Tutorial 1: Introducing Java

The first tutorial (Chapters 1 through 3) covers the basics of Java, including its motivation and design; its operation, syntax, and concepts; and its abilities to handle dynamic extensions to HTML documents, called applets. In Chapter 1, you learn Java's basics through simple examples. You also learn how to create and compile a Java program, and how to use the Java runtime system. In Chapter 2, you learn how to install Java, and how and where to obtain Java. You also write your first, small Java program. In Chapter 3, you tackle your first real programming assignment as you build your very own Java applet.

At the end of this tutorial, you will understand Java's basic structure, its syntax and semantics, and the essentials of its operation and runtime behavior. You also will have developed an appreciation for its extensibility and flexibility as a programming language.

Tutorial 2: Of Applets and Applications

The second tutorial (Chapters 4 and 5) covers the ins and outs of adding a Java applet to an HTML document, and how existing applets can be extended to add new functionality. This tutorial also covers the basics of Java applications—including a compare-and-contrast analysis between applications and applets—and an overview of the application design process. At the end of this section, you will understand what's involved in using and extending Java applets, and what's behind the design and coding of Java applications.

Tutorial 3: Advanced Java Application Science

The final tutorial (Chapters 6 through 10) takes an in-depth look at building and extending Java applications, including what's involved in compiling and running such applications, how they can be extended, and how networking functionality can be used effectively in such applications. This section begins with step-by-step instructions on how to compile and use Java applications. It then moves to a discussion of how such applications can be extended and provides a rationale to help you decide when redefining old objects is preferable to extending them. The application adventure concludes with the requirements analysis for, and the design and implementation of, a Java-based protocol handler.

After a look at these implementation-focused subjects, we turn speculative and discuss Java's potential (along with recommended applications), its shortcomings, and future research and implementation directions. Throughout, we use concrete examples and point to readily accessible Web sites wherever possible.

How to Use this Book

This book tells you what Java is all about and how it works, including the language's keywords, syntax, and construction. Then it tells you what's involved in rendering and using Java. After that, you explore both applets and applications in detail to get a flavor of what Java can do, and how it can be used to extend HTML documents or to make Web-based environments dynamic and open ended.

When you enter fragments of Java code (or whole programs) into your own text editor, be sure to copy the information exactly as you see it in the book. We've tested all this code to make sure it works properly.

We also recommend that you obtain the right set of Java code libraries and their runtime environment before you try to write too much Java code. When appropriate, we try to point out sources for such tools and to share our experiences in using them and their results.

Remember, this book is intended more as an overview of Java and a discussion of its present capabilities and future potential than as a reference for programming. You'll find no shortage of references to on-line resources for programming information in this book, but you'll find neither a comprehensive programming manual, nor complete syntax diagrams, keyword lists, or other tools that you would expect from more detailed training tools.

Where to Go from Here

Like all of the 60 Minute Guides, each part of this book on Java builds on what comes before it. Therefore, we strongly recommend that you set about three hours aside and spend one of those hours on each of the three parts of this book. The book will make a great deal more sense if you read all three parts in their order of occurrence.

After an initial pass through the materials, we expect that you'll find the on-line resources presented throughout the book particularly useful. To help you deal with the specialized terms we use, you'll find a comprehensive glossary to help you figure out what words like *object* and *instance* mean within Java's particular context. You'll not only find yourself revisiting a nice chunk of network programming terminology, you'll probably even expand your vocabulary along the way—at least we did!

Be sure to visit our book's appendixes too:

- Appendix A, entitled The Java System API, describes the various packages, objects, and methods included in the language's application programming interface. This is far from exhaustive, but it does provide a useful overview of how to make system calls within Java, and provides information about call parameters and their basic capabilities.

- Appendix B, entitled Java Language Grammar, provides a pseudo-BNF notation that formally describes the Java language, a reference for those who seek to understand Java's structure and syntax.

But whatever you do, please enjoy this book and the material it covers. Feel free to share your comments and criticisms with us. Our e-mail addresses appear in About the Authors.

Section
One

Introducing Java

Section 1, which includes Chapters 1 through 3, represents the first of three 60-minute tutorials. In this section, we cover the basics of Java, including its primary characteristics and design; its structure, syntax, and concepts; and the ins and outs of writing Java applets. By the time you finish this tutorial, you will have a good idea about what Java is, what it can do, and why it's an incredible leap forward for World Wide Web programming and capability.

In Chapter 1, The Basics of Java, we cover Java's guiding implementation and design principles. Here, you learn that Java is an object-oriented, distributed programming language that is both interpreted and compiled, is architecture neutral, and is portable, multithreaded, and dynamic. You also learn the basic vocabulary and concepts for object-oriented programming and design.

In Chapter 2, The Java Language, you are formally introduced to the language. Here, you learn about Java's basic characteristics, its object orientation, and the various classes, types, and attributes supplied in its built-in object definitions. You'll also come to appreciate Java's control structures, its operators and syntax, and how the language is put together to build programs.

Finally, in Chapter 3, Writing a Java Applet, you encounter the language's more sophisticated side. Here, you learn about its applet variables, constructors, and methods, and about the automatic start-up and shut-down methods that the HotJava browser handles for all Java applets. You also tackle the design and implementation of a small and useful Java applet, one that builds a standard footer for HTML documents.

By the end of this tutorial, you'll have a good idea of what the Java language looks like, how it represents a variety of logical and networking objects, and how it handles variables, instances, classes, and methods. With all of this information under your belt, you'll also have an appreciation for what Java can do, and how it does it!

## CHAPTER 1

The Basics of Java

*n*o doubt about it! Though Java is a new kid on the programming language block, it's hot! Sun Microsystems Inc.'s announcement of Java and the rush of early developers to take advantage of its capabilities already indicate that it fills definite needs for the World Wide Web (WWW, or the Web) community.

That's because Java provides the capability for clients to run applications locally, through hyperlinks in Web pages, that would otherwise have to run remotely on a Web server. This may not sound radical, but it allows all kinds of things to happen on Web clients with Java runtime environments that might not otherwise be possible. Because these things include capabilities such as local search of data, local animation of images, and a wide variety of programmatic extensions to HTML's capabilities, it's no wonder that companies like Netscape Communications and Quarterdeck plan to include Java capabilities in their Web browsers, and that Java-capable browsers, like Sun's own HotJava, are the current rage among sophisticated Internauts.

HotJava?

For clarity's sake, we want to inform you right up front that HotJava is Sun's boldest demonstration of Java technology. It's a Java-enabled Web browser that knows how to handle Java applications and applets, written in Java to show what kinds of applications Java can support and to provide a working example of what Java applications and applets can do.

In this book, we explain what Java is and how it really works, and demonstrate what kinds of capabilities it can deliver, along with those of the HotJava Web browser. To this end, we explore the syntax and semantics of Java as a programming language, and its class libraries and object representation capabilities. To enable you to understand and program in Java, we also provide lots of examples and illustrations to demonstrate its expressive power and capability.

The Java Programming Language

The Java programming language allows you to build both *applets*— nuggets of networked software included in HTML documents—and stand-alone *applications*. Both of these are kinds of Java programs that require you to write Java source code in a text editor just like you would write a C or C++ program. These programs are then compiled using the Java compiler into a binary bytecode format that can be run within a platform-specific Java runtime environment. No matter what your intentions regarding Java may be, you need to understand the structure and syntax of the Java programming language.

Of Bytecodes and Virtual Machines

The Java compiler creates a "binary bytecode format" to execute within a "platform-specific Java runtime environment." There's a lot of beauty, power, and capability buried in these two phrases.

A bytecode format is essentially an intermediate form of code; that is, it has been broken down from a relatively short set of Java language statements to a longer set of intermediate machine instructions that are almost ready to execute on a computer. In other words, the bytecode format includes a large part of the tokenizing and code generation work that an ordinary compiler must also perform, except that it stops short of adopting a machine language targeted for a specific type of computer and operating system.

That's where the runtime environment comes into play. The Java runtime environment takes the 80% completely compiled code produced by the Java compiler and adds the missing 20% that's platform dependent to allow the code to execute on a particular computer. It does this work on the fly as it reads and interprets Java bytecode. That's why you sometimes hear that Java is both compiled and interpreted.

This structure does impose some performance penalties, since programs compiled for a specific machine are undoubtedly more efficient than those compiled into an intermediate format like Java bytecode. However, this approach confers two amazing advantages that many people think make such inefficiency inconsequential by comparison.

1. It allows developers to build Java applications on any platform that supports Java without having to build separate versions of programs for multiple platforms. For most languages, developing for multiple platforms can be incredibly time consuming.

2. It lets users run Java applets or applications on their platforms as soon as Java runtime environments for their platforms are available.

In this chapter, you learn Java's main characteristics as a computer language. We also present a language overview using simple examples, and conclude with a discussion of the Java runtime environment and how it should be installed.

Java's Primary Characteristics

In this section you learn about Java's characteristics, why each is important, and what problem each characteristic attempts to address.

Java Is Object Oriented

Java is a member of the object-oriented paradigm (OO) for programming languages. Languages that adhere to this paradigm, such as Java and C++, have the same underlying philosophy but differ in syntax and style. In a nutshell, OO languages describe interactions among objects. An object consists of both state and behavior. An object's state consists of data elements and their respective values, and its behavior consists of

5

functions (usually called *methods* in the OO vernacular) that operate on those data elements.

Java and other OO languages provide many advantages over traditional procedural languages. Because an object encapsulates related data and functions into a single cohesive unit, it's easy to locate data dependencies, isolate effects of changes, and perform other maintenance activities. OO languages also provide support for information hiding, whereby access to an object's data can be restricted and provided on a strict need-to-know basis. Thus, information hiding reduces the chances that the methods of other objects may inadvertently (or maliciously) modify the state of an object without permission. Finally and perhaps most importantly, OO languages facilitate reuse. Not only are well-designed objects inherently reusable, new objects can be easily formed by creating subclasses of existing objects, thereby reusing existing code and eliminating redundant implementation, testing, and debugging.

Every language paradigm heavily influences application design. Therefore, systems implemented in Java are typically OO systems. This is not an absolute requirement; it is possible to implement a more traditional procedural or functional design in an OO language. However, it is typical, because an OO design maps more intuitively to an implementation in an OO language.

Like other OO languages, Java supports the notion of an object template. Such a template is called a *class* in Java, as in C++. From a class, multiple objects can be instantiated; in any OO system, you may have many active objects, or instances of a class. Each individual object retains its own internal states and interfaces. This implies that any object has a strong sense of autonomy.

During execution of an OO application, an object may invoke one or more methods to accomplish some task. Methods are initiated by a message sent to an object. Upon receiving a message, an object invokes the appropriate method based on the content of the message. Java uses a simple, single-inheritance mechanism—no multiple inheritance—to build a hierarchy of system objects. That is, unlike a C++ object, a Java object can have at most one parent or superclass.

A primary advantage of Java is that each of its objects is self contained. Therefore, every module is inherently reusable. Each module is also extensible, meaning that programmers can add new procedures and new subclasses to any object.

With Java, you can also decompose a problem into logical, intuitive, and salient objects. OO design approaches a problem from a fundamentally different perspective than traditional procedural or functional design. For example, in a functional design for a program that supports the building of hotrod engines, the design focuses primarily on the tools and tasks (i.e., processes or functions) needed to build a hotrod engine.

By contrast, an OO hotrod engine builder focuses mainly on the engine he or she is building and, secondarily, on the tools to build it. This system could be described from the standpoint of data elements and their defined interfaces rather than from the point of view imposed by the tools in use. If you are new to OO design, these concepts should become clearer as you proceed through the examples in this book. Java's drawbacks are shared with other languages that adhere to the OO paradigm. These challenges typically include the following:

- Substantial message passing can cause high system overhead.

- An OO language may require dynamic method bindings because polymorphism allows multiple definitions of methods sharing a common name, and invocation of such polymorphic methods often cannot be resolved until run time.

- OO languages have their own design methodology and philosophy, requiring programmers and designers to learn a new paradigm, new tools, and new techniques because they support multiple active objects rather than sequentially active objects.

Java has the same basic capabilities as C++, but adds the dynamic method resolution features of Objective C to its arsenal. By eliminating many of the more difficult and obfuscated elements of the C++ language, Java achieves an elegant simplicity, making it much easier to learn and to master.

Java's OO characteristics result in many benefits, including easy extensibility of system objects. For instance, the OO hotrod engine builder could create numerous subclasses of engine, such as 2-stroke and 4-stroke. These subclasses could then be subclassed further into gasoline, methanol, and nitro. Figure 1-1 shows a representative object hierarchy for such an example.

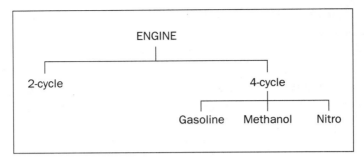

Figure 1-1: Example of engine object hierarchy

Java Is Distributed

Distribution of information for sharing and collaboration, along with distribution of the processing workload, is an essential characteristic of client-server applications. It describes the relationship among system objects that may be on local or remote systems. In the case of the Web, this client-server application takes advantage of both information sharing and workload distribution.

Fortunately for Java programmers, a library of TCP/IP procedures is included in the Java source and binary distribution code. This makes it easy for programmers to access remote information using protocols such as HTTP and FTP. This may be accomplished when a Java application opens a URL to request distributed information from the Web. Other protocols, such as gopher, news, and mailto, are well understood in the WWW world, but have not yet been implemented in the Java language.

Java's distributed behavior enables collaboration and the distribution of system workload. It's also an integral part of client-server architectures, which are distributed by nature. For example, using Java, a distributed OO hotrod engine builder application that supports collaboration from other engine builders in remote locations could be implemented. Using the OO hotrod engine builder, collaborators could work as a team to build a faster and more economical engine.

Java Is Both Interpreted and Compiled

"It's a dessert topping and a floor wax" was first uttered on Saturday Night Live to describe a consumer product with a dual purpose. Well, the same could be said of Java. You compile a Java program into platform-independent binary bytecode form, which is then interpreted by a platform-specific Java runtime environment. Therefore, it's both compiled and interpreted.

What does this buy a developer? Only one source of Java code must be maintained for the compiled bytecode to run in many platform-specific Java environments. For example, you develop a Java program and then compile it. You could then run the same program on a Mac, a PC, or even a UNIX computer, as long as each has a platform-specific Java runtime environment installed—one source, multiple platforms! This allows you to develop applications for the Web faster while pushing the envelopes of functionality and technology.

The Java bytecode binary possesses more compile-time data than is normally available to noninterpreted languages. This information is carried over and made available at runtime, where it can facilitate checks for security and robustness. For example, the linker, which is an integral part of the Java runtime environment, bases its checks on this carried-over data. The Remote Procedure Call (RPC) support included within the Java language is also based on this selfsame carried-over data stream. Finally, carried-over, compile-time information makes debugging easier and more efficient.

What does an interpreted computer language buy you? It relieves developers from worry about the version mismatch problems common to most development environments. By employing the UNIX make tool and resolving inconsistent definitions for module interfaces, this approach allows developers to maintain a single source collection of Java code that easily moves to multiple targets. It also permits information to be incorporated from the runtime environment while a program is being interpreted, thereby supporting dynamic behavior. We cover this in more detail later.

Java Is Architecture Neutral

Java's architecture neutrality is fascinating, but it isn't a new concept. Derived from the Web's distributed client-server nature, an important design feature in Java is support for clients and servers in heterogeneous network configurations. To make sense of the absolute insanity (or seemingly random variability) of the Internet's configurations, a Java bytecode binary object must execute on many different platforms. The method chosen to realize this aim is an *architecture-neutral* binary representation for Java programs.

Such compiled binary objects may be executed in any platform-specific Java runtime environment. Here again, Java requires only one source but can reach many target platforms. Today, WWW software developers usually develop UNIX, then PC, and finally Mac versions of their products. This is not the most productive marketing strategy, and it imposes an exhausting development cycle. Also, the programming staff must be expert in each platform, resulting in a "fat" and specialized work force. Many development hours and much money must be spent to support each platform during its maintenance phase. An architecture-neutral format removes this economic drag and allows developers to concentrate on other aspects of development.

Architecture-neutral bytecode objects contain sterile computer instructions; they possess no allegiance to, or dependence on, a specific computer architecture. Instead, instructions are easy to decipher regardless of platform architecture and may be dynamically converted into any platform's native machine code with relative ease.

Java Is Portable

Java's architecture neutrality characteristic is a big reason why a Java program is portable. Another aspect of portability involves the inherent data structures or types in the language, such as integer, string, and floating point.

Java takes advantage of the IEEE standards for data types common on many types of computers. For instance, in Java a **float** data structure always complies with the IEEE 754 standard for floating-point numbers, while an **int** data type is always a signed twos complement, 32-bit integer. In addition, Java nails down issues related to big-endian and little-endian hardware byte order dependencies. These aspects of Java differ from other languages such as C++ because the Java bytecode binary has no implementation dependence; hence, it's portable to many different platforms.

Following in the portable footsteps of the Java language, the Java runtime environment is also portable. The Java compiler is written in Java itself, while the runtime environment is written in ANSI C and sports a well-defined and succinct portability interface. The POSIX standardization effort was a huge influence on Java's portability interface.

What does portability buy you? Implementing an abstract Java Window class object with its associated methods that will run on a

Mac, PC, and UNIX computer goes straight to the bottom line because it eliminates redundant implementation, testing, and maintenance efforts altogether.

Java Is Multithreaded

Java bytecode binary objects can consist of multiple, simultaneous threads of execution. These are known as either *execution contexts* or *lightweight processes*. C and C++ languages are members of a single-threaded execution paradigm in that they do not provide language-level support for threads. Java, however, provides language-level support for multithreading, resulting in a more multifaceted and powerful approach to programming.

Many things around us happen simultaneously and may not be represented in a strictly sequential fashion. Multithreading, though sometimes difficult to implement, is a method for implementing parallel execution of multiple threads.

Java utilizes a complex set of synchronization primitives first introduced in 1974 by Anthony C. Hoare in the monitor-condition paradigm within operating system theory. Because of the integration of these primitives, the implementation of multithreading in Java programs is straightforward and quite robust. According to the Java language specification, much of the multithreading capability may be attributed to the Xerox Cedar-Mesa system.

What else does multithreading buy you? Users realize real-time behavior and superior interactive responsiveness. For example, you needn't experience the sinking feeling associated with the dreaded hourglass cursor in Microsoft Windows 3.1.

But the Java language specification is quick to point out that these benefits are limited by the runtime computing platform and by reliance on other platform-specific characteristics. For example, if the underlying operating system doesn't support parallel threads, Java's multithreading benefits may not be fully realized. However, a stand-alone Java application that is not limited by the underlying OS can exhibit tremendous real-time responsiveness.

Java Is Dynamic

Dynamic design allows Java programs to adapt to changing computing environments. For example, most typical C++ development relies

11

heavily on class libraries that may be owned and developed by other parties. Many third-party libraries, such as those distributed with an operating system or a windowing system, are linked dynamically and sold or distributed separately from an application that depends on them. When these libraries are updated, existing applications that depend on them may break until they are recompiled and redistributed. This adds yet another cost to software maintenance.

Java avoids this problem by delaying the binding of modules. This allows programmers to take complete advantage of OO paradigm concepts. New methods and instance variables for an existing class in a library can be added without breaking a current program, application, or client.

How is this done? In a nutshell, a Java interface specifies inter-object interaction while excluding any instance variables or implementations of methods. A Java class has a runtime representation that allows programmers to query the type of class (a process known as runtime Type Identification, or RTTI) and to dynamically link the class according to the result of the query. This isn't explicitly provided for in C++. These run-time representations also allow the runtime environment to check data structure casts at compile time as well as at runtime, which provides additional error checking.

> "Double your pleasure, double your fun. With C++, you can have undetected cast problems and memory leaks; in Java, you got none." *Biggus Compilus*

What does dynamic execution buy you? In short, it buys you real plug-and-play software modules.

Java Is Robust

The more robust an application is, the more reliable it is. This is as desirable to software developers as it is to consumers. Most OO languages like Java and C++ are strongly typed. This means that most of the data type checking is performed at compile time rather than at runtime. This avoids many errors and errant conditions in applications. Java, unlike C++, requires explicit method declarations, which increase the reliability of applications.

Implicit declarations, which C++ supports mostly to be backward compatible with C, allow for an end-around. In other words, if a method is implicitly declared, type information isn't available. So, C++'s strong type-checking can be defeated, whereas Java's can't. Finally, the Java linker repeats all compiler type check operations to avoid interface and method version inconsistencies.

The most significant difference between C++ and Java is that Java's pointer paradigm does not support pointer arithmetic. Java implements true arrays rather than linked lists of pointers. With true arrays, boundary or subscripting checks can be performed and can guarantee that memory boundaries cannot be violated, which can result in suspect or invalid data. This means that Java denies you a mechanism to cast an integer value to an integer pointer.

Dynamic languages such as Tcl, Smalltalk, and Lisp are typically considered quite robust because programmers need not worry about memory management and memory corruption. Likewise, Java programmers can also deal fearlessly with memory. Plus, many of these languages, including Java, include garbage collection facilities. These capabilities relieve programmers from the sometimes bewildering and awesome responsibilities inherent in memory management; with Java's built-in garbage collection, memory leaks are completely avoided.

Dynamic languages, including Java, are suitable for rapid application prototyping. Why? For one thing, they don't require developers to make all implementation decisions up front. Although it is an excellent prototyping language, Java differs from other dynamic languages in that it requires developers to define all interface definitions prior to implementation. (This isn't the same as making all implementation decisions up front, but it does require some up-front effort.) This allows the compiler to catch potential mistakes before they occur, guaranteeing proper method invocation.

Robustness provides your application with increased reliability, a no-memory-leak guarantee, and an assurance of proper method invocations. It also guarantees that there are no memory violations, such as referencing an object that a Java application has not explicitly instantiated.

Java Is Secure

Since Java is designed for networked environments, security features received lots of attention. For example, if you execute a binary that you download from the Net, it may be infected with a virus. Java applications are guaranteed to be tamper resistant and virus free because they cannot access system heaps, stacks, or memory. In Java, user authentication is implemented with a public-key encryption methodology. This effectively prevents hackers and crackers from examining protected pieces of information such as account names and passwords.

Java and HotJava: Security, Trust, and Safety

Java is designed for maximum security, trust, and safety. These three concepts are also important to the HotJava browser. Let's look at each of these aspects for both Java and HotJava.

Safety

Java is safe because it possesses no inherent semantics for altering a computing environment. In other words, you cannot write code to modify a program's stack, to alter or access unallocated memory, or to reference objects and their methods without explicit consent from the trusted operating system kernel.

This is a result of Java's lack of pointers and implicit type coercion. It is accomplished by mechanisms that include Java semantics that allow no security modifications on its runtime environment, by the design of the virtual Java machine that blocks invalid memory references, by a lack of data type casting in the language, and by bytecode verification to ensure legal semantics and references.

HotJava handles safety mainly by controlling Java applets. These are loaded with a restrictive class loader named NetClassLoader that rigidly controls access to system-level services. For example, when the File class is called from another class loaded by the NetClassLoader, the File class enforces rigid restrictions on its methods.

HotJava controls file and directory access using applets. For instance, by default, applets can access only system files in two directories on UNIX systems, /tmp/hotjava and ~/.hotjava. Additional files and directories can be added to this list only by modifying the HOTJAVA_READ_PATH and HOTJAVA_WRITE_PATH environment variables. You will learn more about these variables later in this chapter.

Security

Java is secure because memory allocation of new objects is performed explicitly using the *new* operator. Also, the invocation of methods is the only mechanism whereby procedures may be executed. This last feature is part of the OO paradigm. The *new* operator relies on a system-level class named ClassLoader. It strictly enforces security rules on the classes it loads. As a result, the ClassLoader class type is the mediator for the capabilities granted to any class that it instantiates.

HotJava watches applet activities closely. It can modify the functionality of an applet following specific events. For example, the NetClassLoader maintains information about which applets originate inside or outside a firewall, as well as information about any socket or file manipulation by each applet. If something suspicious or unwarranted occurs, HotJava can change the applet's behavior and close potentially open security doors.

Trust

Java offers a ClassLoader class type that can verify a digital signature assigned to a specific class before loading it. This means that classes originating from different systems can be assigned different capabilities. Classes can also query the ClassLoader to determine whether they were called from a trusted class.

HotJava is trusted Java code. The source is made available to the public to foster public confidence in the program. Also, there are plans to assign a digital signature to all trusted browser classes, which should prevent malicious alteration of the browser.

Java Is Simple

A main design goal of Java is to create a language as close to C++ as possible to ensure rapid acceptance in the OO development world. Another design goal is to eliminate obscure and maligned features of C++ that detract from comprehension and add to the confusion that can occur during development, implementation, and maintenance phases of software. These features include overloading operators—operators with more than one semantic interpretation—support for multiple class inheritance, and automatic coercion of data types.

When the designers of Java included garbage collection capabilities, they were forced to make a tradeoff. They relieved programmers of the burden of memory management but increased the complexity of the Java runtime system. Java's garbage collection facility eases the burden of OO programming and contributes heavily to the reduction of inherent source code bugs. Thus, by making the runtime system more complex (which only needs to be implemented once for each platform),

Java's designers could make resulting Java applications simpler and easier to code.

Finally, Java is also simple because it is small. The basic Java interpreter occupies approximately 40K of RAM, excluding the multithreaded support and standard libraries, which require another 175K. Even the combined memory required for all these elements is insignificant when compared to other programming languages and environments.

Here's the infamous "Hello world!" program in Java:

```
class HelloWorld{
    static public void main (Strings args[]) {
        System.out.println("Hello world!");
    }
}
```

What does simplicity buy you? Less time in coding and tracking bugs, and more time solving problems and satisfying customers. Simplicity also allows Java programs to run on computers that offer only small or primitive memory models, such as embedded systems or older computers. Java's simplicity also offers a learning curve that isn't as steep as that of C++ and, therefore, permits shorter training time for new recruits to the language.

Java Offers High Performance

There are many situations in which interpretation of bytecode objects provides acceptable performance. But other circumstances demand higher performance. Java accommodates this by providing runtime translation of bytecodes into native machine code.

The design of the bytecode format takes this fact into consideration. The generation of native machine code is relatively simple, so good machine code is produced. The performance of bytecode that has been translated to native machine code is comparable to that of machine code produced by modern C and C++ compilers.

High performance lets you implement your Web applications in Java as small, fast programs that can significantly extend both client and server capabilities.

A Java Language Overview

In this section, we take our first look at the Java language, including the general structure of a Java program, its available system classes, and its class interface definition.

Program Structure Most Java programs contain one or more compilation objects or units. Each unit contains a package and import statements as well as class and interface declarations. While you can have multiple classes and interfaces per unit, each unit can have at most one public interface and class because this is how the unit will be accessed by other objects in the system. The rest must be private, which can be explicitly declared as private in the class declaration or accepted as the default.

When you use the Java compiler, *javac*, you are compiling Java source code into bytecodes. These bytecodes contain instructions that are machine independent. The Java interpreter, also called *java* and part of the Java runtime environment, then interprets these bytecodes. When creating a Java compilation unit, each must have a *.java* suffix.

The Package Statement A package is a group of classes and interfaces. It is an abstraction of the Java language that allows management of groups of classes while also handling class name contention. Consider a package as a wrapper for multiple classes and interfaces, or as a name for a collection of classes and interfaces. In Java, every class and interface must be contained in a package.

A package name is specified as a list of words separated by a period, with the initial name in the list indicating the class owner and developer.

The Import Statement Java provides a mechanism for including definitions and implementations for classes and interfaces within other packages, namely the *import* keyword. This keyword asserts that external classes are imported into the current package. By default, a compilation unit automatically imports all classes and interfaces contained in a package. For example, the following Java code fragment imports all public classes of the MarkUp package:

```
// import all classes from MarkUp
import MarkUp.*;
```

17

The Class Declaration

A class in the OO paradigm typically maps to a real-world object like an engine, a chair, or a window. A class can also represent intangible objects, such as a transaction or a football game. A class supports data abstraction. When a new class is created using the *new* operator, a sub-class is created from a super class.

In Java, all classes are derived from the system class named Object, and each class except Object has one and only one superclass, where a superclass is the parent of a derived class. Java supports only single inheritance of classes while supporting multiple inheritance of class methods. Through the class interface, Java provides many multiple inheritance mechanisms found in languages such as C++.

A class declaration has the following form. Keywords in brackets are optional:

```
[list of modifiers] class Classname [extends SuperClassname]
[implements Interface{,Interface}] {
... body of class ...
}
```

Here are examples:

```
// create simple class for an applet
class ThatsCool extends Applet {
...
}
// create a two-dimensional point in space
public class 2dPoint {
...
}
// create a renderable two-dimensional point
public class Renderable2DPoint extends Point
    implements Renderable {
...
  }
```

The Interface Declaration

Typical of most OO languages, Java's interface to a class defines a collection of methods while requiring that these methods be implemented. This division of interface and implementation allows OO designs to be rapid, because implementation details can be completed later in an application's life cycle. Another advantage, information hiding, restricts the visibility of instance variables within a class. Java has three levels of information hiding: protected, public, and private. As in C++, public implies global visibility, protected implies visibility within the class and its descendant classes, and private implies visibility only within the class.

Interfaces also provide encapsulation for method protocols. The implementation of these protocols is not restricted to any particular inheritance hierarchy; because they can be referenced in any object that implements the interface, this provides considerable flexibility. Excluding abstract classes—classes declared for common instances but never instantiated—a class must implement all methods whenever programmers construct an interface to that class.

In Java, the class interface has the advantage of reduced runtime overhead in its implementation of multiple-inheritance characteristics found in C++. Another advantage of a class interface is that it hides interface implementation details when shared between classes. Class interfaces do, however, suffer from the following disadvantage: this approach requires dynamic method binding which, in turn, reduces runtime performance.

An interface is declared using the keyword, *interface*. Similar to classes, interfaces are private by default or public by declaration. An interface's methods are always public, while variables for the interface are public and static—that is, available to anyone and not permitted to be changed, renamed, or extended.

The following example supplies the declaration for an interface and the methods that implement it:

```
public interface Access {
    void Badge(Stream a);
    void SignIn(Stream a);
}
public class Security implements Access {
    void Badge(Stream a) {
    ...
    }
    void SignIn(Stream a) {
    ...
    }
}
```

The Java Environment

In this section, you learn about the tools included in the Java distribution from Sun, how to install and set up the Java and HotJava environment, and about Java environment variables. Finally, you will write your first short Java applet to test your new environment.

Currently, the Alpha3 release of Java and HotJava supports only *Sun Solaris 2.3, 2.4,* and *2.5 Sparc-based* machines. The Alpha2 release supports *Microsoft Windows NT 3.5* and *3.51* on Intel x86 machines. Sun is currently porting the Java and HotJava system to Windows 95 and the Macintosh OS (MacOS).

Solaris Installation

The following section details how to obtain the binaries for the Java and HotJava environment for machines supported by the Alpha3 release. The basic purpose of this release is to demonstrate Java concepts.

The following steps download a UNIX compressed tar file that is about 5.5MB in size. After uncompressing and untarring this file, you need about 16MB of disk space (about 11MB if you delete the tar.Z file). There are two different methods for retrieving the Alpha3 release. The simplest way is to open this URL:

```
ftp://java.sun.com/pub/hotjava-alpha3-solaris2-sparc.tar.Z
```

This automatically downloads a UNIX compressed tar file to your machine. You then untar this file as described later in this section.

The other method is to start an anonymous FTP session with either of these sites and their respective paths:

```
sunsite.unc.edu:   pub/sun-info/hotjava/hj-alpha3.tar.Z
java.sun.com:      pub/hotjava-alpha3-solaris2-spar.tar.Z
```

To Start an FTP Session (The % is the UNIX prompt.)

```
% ftp java.sun.com
Connected to java.sun.com.
220 java FTP server (Version wu-2.4(5) Fri Jul 14 10:19:52 PDT 1995)
ready.
```

```
Name (java.sun.com:demo): anonymous
331 Guest login ok, send your complete e-mail address as password.
Password: demo@hal.com
[ ... information header omitted ...]
ftp> binary
200 Type set to I.
ftp> cd pub
250 CWD command successful.
ftp> get hotjava-alpha3-solaris2-sparc.tar.Z
200 PORT command successful.
150 Opening BINARY mode data connection for hotjava-alpha3-solaris2-
sparc.tar.Z
(5476079 bytes).
226 Transfer complete.
local: hotjava-alpha3-solaris2-sparc.tar.Z remote: hotjava-alpha3-
solaris2-sparc.tar.Z
5476079 bytes received in 1e+02 seconds (43 Kbytes/s)
ftp> quit
```

Untarring the Release After the download is complete and successful, you must untar it. On the command line, enter this command:

```
% zcat hotjava-alpha3-solaris2-sparc.tar.Z | tar xvf -
```

This creates a directory named *hotjava* in the current directory. This command also retains the UNIX compressed tar file in case you need to extract original files from it. If disk space is tight, delete the compressed tar file.

Running HotJava Launch the HotJava browser with this command:

```
% hotjava/bin/hotjava &
```

This executes the hotjava binary in the background from the release binary directory. You can also add the path for the **hotjava** binary to your environment's path as in this C shell example. The example assumes that the **hotjava** release is in a directory named /u/share/.

```
set path = ($path /u/share/hotjava/bin)
```

After altering your path variable, enter:

```
% source ~/.cshrc
```

21

This makes the new path available to the shell. Now, to run HotJava, simply enter:

```
% hotjava &
```

For more information about the Solaris release, see this URL:

```
http://java.sun.com/installation-alpha3-solaris2-sparc.html
```

The Windows NT Installation

The current Alpha2 release of Java and HotJava supports only Windows NT 3.5 and 3.51 on Intel x86 computers. The following section details how to obtain the binaries for the Java and HotJava environment. The basic purpose of this alpha release is to demonstrate Java concepts.

To run HotJava and Java under Windows NT, you need:

- an x86 Intel computer running Windows NT 3.5 or 3.51 that supports long file names on a File Allocation Table (FAT) partition
- 8-bit color (other color depths are not supported)
- a 16-bit SoundBlaster card

The following steps download a self-extracting archive file that is about 3.6MB in size. After extracting the file, you need about 11MB of disk space. There are two different methods for retrieving the Alpha2 release. The simplest way is to open this URL:

```
ftp://java.sun.com/pub/hotjava-alpha2-nt-x86.exe
```

This automatically downloads a self-extracting archive file to your machine. You can then run the self-extracting archive executable on your machine.

The other method is to start an anonymous FTP session to this site and its path:

```
java.sun.com: pub/hotjava-alpha2-nt-x86.exe
```

To Start an FTP Session

```
% ftp java.sun.com
Connected to java.sun.com.
220 java FTP server (Version wu-2.4(5) Fri Jul 14 10:19:52 PDT 1995)
ready.
Name (java.sun.com:demo): anonymous
331 Guest login ok, send your complete e-mail address as password.
```

```
Password: demo@hal.com
[ ... information header omitted ...]
ftp> binary
200 Type set to I.
ftp> cd pub
250 CWD command successful.
ftp> get hotjava-alpha2-nt-x86.exe
200 PORT command successful.
150 Opening BINARY mode data connection for hotjava-alpha2-nt-x86.exe
(3618772 bytes).
226 Transfer complete.
local: hotjava-alpha2-nt-x86.exe remote: hotjava-alpha2-nt-x86.exe
3618772 bytes received in 1e+02 seconds (36 Kbytes/s)
ftp> quit
```

Extracting the Archive After the download is complete and successful, you must run the self-extracting archive file. This can be done through Program Manager or from the command line in a DOS window:

```
hotjava-alpha2-nt-x86
```

This command creates a subdirectory named **hotjava** in the current directory. It also retains the self-extracting archive file in case you need to extract original files from the release. If disk space is tight, delete the self-extracting archive file.

Running HotJava Launch the HotJava browser with this command:

```
hotjava\bin\hotjava
```

This executes the hotjava binary from the release binary directory. You can also add the path to the hotjava binary to your environment's path in your AUTOEXEC.BAT file. The following assumes that the hotjava release is in a directory named \u\share\:

```
PATH=$PATH:\u\share\hotjava\bin
```

For more information about the Windows NT release, see this URL:

```
http://java.sun.com/installation-alpha2-nt-x86.html
```

This URL also contains information about troubleshooting your installation. It is not included here because it changes rapidly and would be out of date by the time you read it.

Alpha3 Release Source Code

The full source code for the Alpha3 release of Java and HotJava is available through anonymous *FTP*. You are required to read the licensing agreement and to complete an HTML form with information before the source code is released to you.

Information about the source release FAQ, the licensing agreement, porting information, and the source form and instructions are found at this URL:

```
http://java.sun.com/source.html
```

Other Platforms

Ports are under development for Windows 95 and the MacOS 7.5 operating systems. For status and release information, join Sun's external mailing lists for Java and HotJava. For more information about these mailing lists, check this URL:

```
http://java.sun.com/mail.html
```

Testing Your Installation

Now we'll test your installation of Java and HotJava by writing a simple Java application for UNIX. But before you begin, you need to create two directories. First, create a directory to hold your HTML documents. For our examples this will be /u/demo/html.

```
% mkdir /u/demo/html
```

Next, create a subdirectory called *classes* to store your *.java* applets and applications. The Java compiler, *javac*, will also create class instances in this directory with a *.class* extension.

```
% mkdir /u/demo/html/classes
```

Your First Java Application This section outlines the steps to create your first stand-alone Java application.

1. Using your favorite text editor, enter the following Java code:

```
// This is an example Java standalone application. It
// displays the current system date and time.
// Import from the system java.util package
// a class named Date.
```

```
import java.util.Date;

class DateApplication {
    public static void main (String args[]) {
        Date current = new Date();
        System.out.println(current);
    }
}
```

2. Save file as DateApplication.java in the /u/demo/html/classes/ directory.

3. Run the java compiler on the application:

```
% javac DateApplication.java
```

This creates a file in the /u/demo/html/classes directory named DateApplication.Class.

4. Run the java interpreter on the new class:

```
% java DateApplication
Thu Jul 20 16:36:34 CDT 1995
```

Congratulations, you have just written your first Java application!

Your First Java Applet The following steps show how to create your first Java applet, which will be invoked from an HTML document.

1. Using your favorite text editor, enter the following Java code:

```
/* This is an example Java applet. It displays the current system date
and time rendered into an HTML document. */

// Import from the system java.util package a class named Date
import java.util.Date;
// Import a class from the system browser package
import browser.Applet;
// Import a Graphics class from the system awt package
import awt.Graphics;

// define a new subclass
class DateApplet extends Applet{
    // assign current system date to private class variable
    Date current = new Date();
```

25

```
    // define method called by HotJava by default
    public void init() {
        // set the size of the rendered string
        resize(200,25);
    }
    // define a method to paint the browser canvas
    public void paint(Graphics g) {
        // convert the current system date to a string
        String s = current.toString();
        /* render the string in the browser at the coordinates */
        g.drawString(s,5,25);
    }
}
```

2. Save this source code as a file named DateApplet.java in the /u/demo/html/classes/ directory.

3. Run the java compiler on the application:

```
% javac DateApplet.java
```

This creates a file in the /u/demo/html/classes directory named DateApplet.class.

4. Use your text editor to create the following HTML document:

```
<!DOCTYPE HTML PUBLIC "-//IETF//DTD HTML//EN">
<HTML>
<HEAD>
<TITLE>Java Date Applet</TITLE>
</HEAD>
<BODY>
<H1>Java Date Applet</H1>

<P>System Date:
<!--identify object to run as applet -->
<APP CLASS="DateApplet">

</BODY>
</HTML>
```

5. Save this HTML document as date.html in the /u/demo/html/ directory.

6. In HotJava, open the location:

```
file:/u/demo/html/date.html
```

Congratulations, you have now written your first Java applet and invoked it from inside an HTML document!

The Java Environment Tools

The Java environment is made up of many tools that include the following elements:

- *java*—the interpreter that runs Java programs in bytecode form
- *javac*—the Java compiler that compiles Java source code into bytecode
- *hotjava*—the WWW client written in Java
- *javah*—creates header files and stub files so you can implement native methods for any class
- *javap*—disassembles bytecode into Java source code
- *javadoc*—automatically generates HTML documents from Java source code
- *javaprof*—pretty-prints profiling information for single-threaded applications

Environment Variables

HotJava lets you define a set of environment variables to tailor HotJava to meet system constraints or requirements.

WWW_HOME If the WWW_HOME variable is set, it specifies a default Welcome page. Upon launching HotJava for the first time, a URL can be specified on the command line to which it then loads and renders. If HotJava is executed without a URL, it retrieves and renders either:

- the value of the environment variable WWW_HOME, or
- file://~/demo/, if WWW_HOME is not set.

The value of WWW_HOME may be either a URL or a Java *doc* resource. Here is a typical URL specification for WWW_HOME in a C shell:

```
setenv WWW_HOME "http://www.hal.com/"~markg/"
```

Here is an example of the value pointing to a Java resource document:

```
setenv WWW_HOME "doc:///doc/index.html"
```

HOTJAVA_HOME The HOTJAVA_HOME variable sets where HotJava scans for resources it requires to execute. The default value is the directory where the release was initially installed on your system. This example sets HOTJAVA_HOME to another directory:

```
setenv HOTJAVA_HOME /hotjava
```

HOTJAVA_READ_PATH HOTJAVA_READ_PATH determines whether an applet has permission to read a file from the file system. This supplies one level of built-in security in HotJava. Each applet is allowed to read files only from matched directories and their subdirectories, and files that match a resource *exactly*. Its value is specified as a list of directories or files separated by colons. By default, this variable takes the value of the installation directory, which is /hotjava/ in the following example:

```
/hotjava/:$HOME/html/:$HOME/images
```

This specification allows HotJava applets to read files from three directories: the default installation directory, the user's public HTML directory, and the user's images directory. Following the previous example, an applet can read a file from the directory:

```
$HOME/images/personal/
```

To avoid this, alter the value to read:

```
setenv HOTJAVA_READ_PATH /hotjava/:$HOME/html/:$HOME/images/public
```

Now, an applet can read images from the *public* subdirectory but not from the *personal* subdirectory, because the value will not match the applet's request.

You can also bypass this security measure altogether by setting this variable's value to "*" (double quotes are required). For example:

```
setenv HOTJAVA_READ_PATH "*"
```

This disables any checking of read permissions by any applet. But because it makes the variable invisible, it's not recommended.

HOTJAVA_WRITE_PATH HOTJAVA_WRITE_PATH is used by HotJava to decide if an applet has permission to write to a file. Its value is a list of directories or files separated by colons. By default, its value is:

```
/tmp/:/devices/:/dev/:~/.hotjava
```

If an applet wants to write to a file, HotJava determines if the file matches any of the directories or files in the value of this variable.

To disable this level of security on applets, set the value of the variable to "*" (double quotes are required). For example:

```
setenv HOTJAVA_WRITE_PATH "*"
```

Because it's a good idea to maintain this security, disabling all applet security is definitely not recommended.

CLASS_PATH CLASS_PATH is used by the *javac* compiler, the *java* interpreter, *javah* (which creates C header and stub files), the *javap* class disassembler, and *javadoc* (which generates an HTML document from a Java source file). Only *hotjava* and *javaprof* don't used this variable, which provides a path to user-defined classes in the system. Its value is a list of directories separated by colons. For example:

```
setenv CLASS_PATH .:/html/classes:/export/java/classes
```

Industry-Wide Acceptance of Java and HotJava

Sun Microsystems, Inc., aggressively promoting Java and HotJava, recently revealed its earliest users. In Sunnyvale, CA, **Mitsubishi Electric** is working on embedded systems written in Java. In Japan, **Fuji Xerox** has been developing Java programs since mid-1994. In Palo Alto, CA, **Andersen Consulting** is currently developing publishing, communication, and financial applications. In Columbus, Ohio, the Internet division of **CompuServe** plans to support applets in its Mosaic WWW client when Windows 95 ships. **Eastman Kodak** plans to use HotJava to deliver to consumers an on-line inventory of digital images and video. Other institutions planning to utilize HotJava are information providers such as **HotWired, Dimension X**, and **Starwave Inc.**, and advertising entities **MediaShare Corp.** and **Foote, Cone, and Belding.**

In May, 1995, **Netscape Communications Corp.** announced plans to license Java for their Navigator WWW browser. Netscape intends to support the Java language within HTML documents and license the Java runtime environment, the Java compiler, and other Java development tools.

Summary

Java augments the existing tools suite for today's OO programmers. Since Java adheres to the OO paradigm, programming is easier because compilation units can be mapped to real-world objects. In addition, Java's garbage collection facilities lessen programming effort. Finally, because compiled Java bytecode is architecture neutral, the diversity of the Internet is finally addressed directly within a powerful, OO programming language.

Now that you've seen the broad outlines of Java, you're probably curious about what's under the hood. Be patient! We'll start your guided tour of the language and its syntax in the next chapter.

## CHAPTER 2

The Java | Language

*i*n this chapter, we look at the gory details of the Java language. Java is quite similar to C++, so seasoned veterans should fly through this chapter, while neophytes might need to invest a little more time. After this chapter, you will be able to read complex Java source code and walk away with a basic understanding of what it means. This chapter sufficiently acquaints you with Java syntax and constructs to let you write your first complex Java program. You learn about lexical token concepts in the Java language as well as inherent data types, classes, interfaces, packages, expressions, and statements.

Tokens

We begin by examining the lexical issues in the Java language. The tokens resulting from a lexical analysis from the Java scanner may be classified as: identifiers, keywords, literals, operators, and separators. After they are identified by the scanner, the tokens are passed to the Java parser for syntax and semantic analysis.

Comments

But before we tear into the identifiers, you need to learn what constitutes a valid Java comment. Comments in Java can be specified in three different ways. The first two are taken from C++ and C. The third is a specialized comment that can immediately precede any declaration. Here's the syntax:

```
// text, which may not span more than one line
/* text */
/** text */
```

Here are examples:

```
// This is a single-line Java comment gleaned from C++
/* This is a Java comment inherited from C */
/** This is a specialized comment that can immediately precede any
declaration */
```

The last comment specification identifies text for inclusion in the automatic generation of documentation from the source code file and will serve as the description of that declared entity supplied as documentation.

Identifiers

A Java identifier must start with a letter (a-z, A-Z), an underscore (_), or a dollar sign ($). Characters following the initial character can also contain digits (0-9). Java incorporates the Unicode character set, based on the Unicode Standard, Worldwide Character Encoding, version 1.0, volumes 1 and 2.

A valid Java identifier can contain the following characters:

- characters in the set (a-z, A-Z)
- all Unicode characters above the hexadecimal number 00C0, which excludes some special characters

Here are valid examples:

```
chevelle
_454-LS-5
$poteau
Bjørn
sçron
```

For more information about the Unicode character set, see this URL:

```
http://www.stonehand.com/unicode.html
```

Keywords

Java includes a set of identifiers reserved as keywords. No keyword may be used other than as dictated by the Java language. The following is a list of the keywords:

abstract	continue	for	new	switch
boolean	default	goto*	null	synchronized
break	do	if	package	this
byte	double	implements	private	threadsafe
byvalue*	else	import	protected	throw
case	extends	instanceof	public	transient
catch	false	int	return	true
char	final	interface	short	try
class	finally	long	static	void
const*	float	native	super	while

* designates reserved, but not implemented yet.

Literals

Java has five literal types: integer, floating point, Boolean, character, and string.

Character Java provides character literals, which can be a single character or a group of characters that represent a single character. These literals are of type **char** and are members of the Unicode character set. A character is represented as an unsigned 16-bit integer. Table 2-1 specifies those escape sequences that represent common nongraphical characters.

Table 2-1: Escape Sequences for Common Nongraphical Characters

DESCRIPTION	CHARACTER	ESCAPE SEQUENCE
Unicode char	0xdddd	\uddd
octal char	0ddd	\ddd
hexadecimal char	0xdd	\xdd
backslash	\	\\
single quote	'	\'
double quote	"	\"
carriage return	CR	\r

Table 2-1: *Continued*

DESCRIPTION	CHARACTER	ESCAPE SEQUENCE
new line	NL or LF	\n
formfeed	FF	\f
backspace	BS	\b
continuation	<new line>	\
horizontal tab	HT	\t

A "d" represents a digit in the table.

String Java provides a string literal, which is a series of zero or more characters contained within double quotes. Java represents this type of literal in a very different way from C++. In C++, a string is an array of characters. In Java, a string literal is implemented as an object of type **String**. For example, this Java fragment creates a new instance of the class **String**:

```
String name = "Stirling";
```

Here are examples of valid **string** literals:

```
"Go hard, fast, and wild."
"Go hard, fast, \
and wild on two lines."
"" // an empty string
"\"Ciao!\"" // string literal for "Ciao!"
```

Boolean Java provides the two obvious literal values of true and false for Boolean values. These values are *not* strings and cannot be coerced to a **String** literal type.

Integer Java provides three representations for an **integer** literal: octal (base 8), decimal (base 10), and hexadecimal (base 16). An octal **integer** literal starts with a leading zero and is followed by a series of digits ranging from 0 to 7. A decimal **integer** literal comprises a series of digits (0-9), but may not contain a leading zero. A hexadecimal **integer** literal starts with a zero followed by an X or x (0X or 0x), followed by a series of digits from 0 to 9, or letters from "a" to "f" or "A" to "F." **Integer** literals are of type **int** if they are represented in 32 bits or less. **Integer** literals that require more than 32 bits to represent them are of type **long**. You can make a regular **integer** literal into a **long** type by appending a lowercase or uppercase L to the series of digits.

Here are valid **integer** literals:

```
13L
0
027
0XBaDbAd
```

Floating Point **Floating-point** literals in Java are composed of the following components: a base-10 integer, a decimal point, a fraction (which is a series of base-10 integers), an exponent (uppercase or lowercase E followed by a signed base-10 integer), and a type designator (which is a character literal). A **floating-point** literal must have at least one digit plus a decimal point or an uppercase or lowercase E. Java has two representations or types for floating-point literals. The first is for single-precision floating-point literals, which are type **float**. Double-precision floating-point literals are type **double**. **double** should be used when calculations are mission critical. Both of these types are based on the IEEE 754 standard for floating-point numbers.

Here are examples of valid floating-point literals:

```
/* Single precision floating-point literals of type float */
4.5
4.5f
4.5F
4.5e12
/* Double precision floating-point literals of type double */
4.5d
4.5D
4.556677De101766
```

Operators and Separators

Java provides reserved characters and character combinations that represent operators and separators. Here's a list:

+	-	!	%	^	&	*
|	~	/	>	<	(	)
{	}	[	]	;	?	:
,	.	=	++	—	==	<=
>=	!=	<<	>>	>>>	+=	-=
*=	/=	&=	|=	^=	%=	<<=
>>=	>>>=	||	&&			

Types

Typical of programming languages, every Java variable or expression is represented as a type. That is, it possesses a defined type attribute. A type provides the legal range of values for a variable or expression. This means that a determination can be made from a variable's type about the allowable range of values that variable can store and the set of operations allowed on those values. As a result, Java provides built-in types. It also permits programmers to create new, user-defined types using the interface and classes based on the intrinsic system **Class** type.

Java provides atomic types—singular-base types that cannot be reduced any further—and composite types, which are constructed from atomic types. In this section, you learn about the atomic types: **integer**, **floating point**, **character**, and **Boolean**. You also learn about the intrinsic composite types: **array**, **interface**, and **class**.

Integer

Java provides a unique representation for the **integer** type because of the language's design goal to be machine independent. While this is different from the integer representation model for C and C++, integers in Java are quite similar to C and C++ integers in other respects.

There are four types of integers in Java, all of which are signed and can have 8-, 16-, 32-, or 64-bit representations. Table 2-2 depicts the four **integer** types and their respective names.

The **integer** type determines the range of values and the set of legal operations on the values. It does not impose a storage model because of the machine independence of Java bytecodes.

Table 2-2: The Four Integer Types in Java

Bit Representation	Type Name
8	byte
16	short
32	int
64	long

Here are examples of valid integer variable declarations in Java:

```
byte count;   // 8-bit integer
short count;  // 16-bit integer
int count;    // 32-bit integer
long count;   // 64-bit integer
```

Floating Point

To designate a 32-bit, single-precision floating-point type in Java, the **float** keyword is required. For a 64-bit, double-precision floating-point type, the **double** keyword is required.

If both operands of a binary operation are type **float**, the result is also type **float**. If one of the operands is type **double**, the result of the operation is type **double**.

Here are examples of valid floating-point variable declarations:

```
float result;     /* 32-bit, single-precision floating point */
double fraction;  /* 64-bit, double-precision floating point */
```

Boolean

Java provides a **Boolean** type, which is utilized for variables, for return values of methods with either a true or false value, and for return values of relational operations such as the less-than operator (<). The **Boolean** keyword is required.

Here are examples of valid Boolean variable declarations:

```
boolean found;
boolean status = true;
```

Boolean values are not numbers like those found in C and C++, and cannot be coerced into integers by casting.

Character

Java provides a **character** type based on the Unicode character set. The **char** keyword is required, and this type is represented as an unsigned 16-bit integer.

Here are valid character type variable declarations:

```
char percent_sign = '%';
char carriage_return = '\012'; // octal representation
```

Array

In Java, arrays are instances of subclasses of the class **Object**. For every primitive type such as **char**, **int**, or **float**, you can create an associated subclass of type **Array**. Java considers arrays as first-class objects that cannot be subclassed. So you will not find a class definition of interface, methods, and instance variables for the class **Array** in the system class library.

The **Array** class has an instance variable named **length**. This variable is equal to the number of entries in an **Array**. Subscripting starts at zero for Java arrays. For example, the following Java fragment prints the number 5, which is the number of allocated entries in the integer array, to the STDOUT logical device.

```
int a[] = new int[5];
System.out.println(a.length);
```

Array also replaces pointer arithmetic found in C and C++. Arrays, as well as all other objects, are referenced by Java pointers that cannot be mistakenly or maliciously compromised by manipulation. This is one of Java's nicest features, and eliminates memory leaks and memory corruption.

Arrays are created using the **new** operator, which is required every time you allocate or create an array. You cannot specify the intended dimension or length of the array on the left-hand side of the assignment, the **lvalue**. The length must be specified on the right-hand side of the assignment. For example, this Java fragment creates a *new* instance of the **Array** class for integer types with a length of 25 elements:

```
int elements[] = new int[25];
```

Arrays of more than one dimension are not supported by Java, but can be implemented as arrays of arrays. You must provide at least one dimension. Other dimensions can be allocated later in your Java code. Here are some examples:

```
int elements[] = new int[40][55];
int elements[] = new int[30][]; /* 2nd dimension to be allocated later */
```

Finally, Java guarantees security by rigidly checking array subscript boundaries. If an array has an out-of-bounds subscript, an **ArrayIndexOutOfBoundsException** is raised and the program terminates. Array subscripts must be valid integer expressions. Here are valid examples:

```
int a[] = new int[20];
a[2] = 123;
a[1] = a[2] + a[4] + a[19];
```

Here are some examples in which the subscripts are out of bounds and raise an exception at run time:

```
a[-3] = 4321; // raises ArrayIndexOutOfBoundsException
a[20] = 1;    // raises ArrayIndexOutOfBoundsException
```

The last example is invalid because the subscript range is 0-19—a length of 20—but the indexing of arrays begins at zero.

Classes

A class combined with an interface provides the base concept in the OO paradigm. A class is a template used to create (instantiate) objects, or instances of a class, and defines the behavior and state of an object. The object might represent something in the real world, or an imaginary or hypothetical object (e.g., the electrical constant *i*, used to model the square root of -1). An object is a way to describe data in specific terms; classes are modeled after objects from the problem domain, such as Window, String, and Point.

Each class in Java is derived from the mother of all classes, the **Object** class. Derivation is also called subclassing. Each and every class has exactly one superclass, except for the **Object** class. If a new class is declared without specifying its superclass, the **Object** class is the default superclass. For example, these two new class declarations are equivalent:

```
class Foo {
   ... body of class ...
}
class Foo extends Object {
   ... body of class ...
}
```

One class in particular, the **Array** class, cannot be subclassed. It is considered a first-class entity. For example, this is invalid Java code:

```
class MyArray extends Array {
   ... body of class ...
}
```

In general, a class provides an OO mechanism to accommodate abstraction, information hiding, and encapsulation of data and methods. Keywords such as **protected**, **public**, and **private** provide controlled access mechanisms to class variables and methods.

A new class must be derived from an existing class. This new class is also known as a derived subclass of a superclass. For example, the **String** class is a subclass of the **Object** class. If you create a new class called **MyString** that specializes **String**, you must make the new class a subclass of the **String** class. The subclass inherits all the **public** and **protected** methods and instance variables of its superclass. Inheritance continues up the class hierarchy until reaching the base class, **Object**.

You can also specialize your new class by adding new functionality or behavior. Finally, derivation of a class from a superclass is transitive. For example, if Dog is a subclass of Animal and Chow is a subclass of Dog, then Chow is a subclass of Animal.

Syntax and Structure

The class declaration has the following syntax, which we saw briefly in Chapter 1. (Keywords in brackets are optional.)

```
[list of modifiers] class Classname [extends SuperClassname]
[implements Interface{,Interface}] {
  [instance variables]
  ... methods declarations ...
}
```

Let's look at an example:

```
/* Import the system package named browser and all its classes */
import browser.*;


/* This declares a new class named Forty-Two. It is derived from the
system class browser.Applet and implements a system-defined interface
named Runnable. */
class Forty-Two extends Applet implements Runnable {
  String s; // instance variable
  int I;    // instance variable
  ... methods ...
}
```

Casting of Classes

Java provides the capability to cast one type as another type. Since each new class is a new type, Java supports casting between these new types. The syntax for casting is:

```
(classname)variable
```

For example, if Dog is a subclass of Animal, then an instance of Dog can be referenced and utilized as an instance of type Animal. An explicit cast is valid in Java, but is not required. This is called *widening* of a class. Here's the code for the above example:

```
// class declaration for Animal
class Animal {
  String id = "animal";
}
// class declaration for Dog
class Dog extends Animal {
  String id = "dog";
}
class Example {
  void test {
    Dog d = new Dog(); // create a new Dog instance
    System.out.println(d.id); // print "dog" to STDOUT

    Animal a;
    a = (Animal)d;  // cast Dog instance "d" as Animal
    System.out.println(a.id); // print "animal" to STDOUT
  }
}
```

You can also *narrow* a class by casting it to a subclass. These are checked at run time to validate that the class and subclass are directly related in class hierarchy. You cannot cast among sibling classes, which results in a runtime error.

Instance Variables

An instance variable is any nonstatic variable of a class declared outside the scope of any method in the class. Instance variables can have modifiers typical of those in C and C++, but with a few additions. Table 2-3 summarizes these new modifiers.

Table 2-3: Java Variable Modifiers

Keyword	Description
threadsafe	instance or static variable; cannot change asynchronously
transient	flags interpreter that object is persistent
final	class cannot have subclass; method cannot be overridden; variable has constant value
native	method implemented in machine-dependent language
abstract	superclass or interface; defines a protocol that subclass must implement
synchronized	method or block of code; requires a lock before execution

Instance variables may be of any type and may have initializers. By default, numeric instance variables are equal to zero, Boolean variables are equal to false, and objects are initialized as null. Initializers are the same as in C or C++, as shown in this example:

```
class Dog {
   String id = "DogClass"; /* instance variable initialized */
}
```

this and *super* Variables

Java provides two special variables, **this** and **super**. **this** references the current object declared within the scope of a nonstatic method. (Static methods, because they are owned by classes rather than objects, cannot reference the **this** or **super** variables. Static methods are explained later in this chapter.) This Java code fragment has an object pass itself as a parameter to another object:

```
class Goo {
  /* method with one parameter that is another class, "soo" */
  void test (soo s) {
    s.playit(this); /* pass current object to "soo" type object */
  }
}
```

Instance variables can also be referenced with a **this** variable, although it is implied and isn't necessary. For instance, this fragment prints the same value for the *soo* variable twice:

```
class Goo {
  int soo = 101;
  void test () {
    System.out.println(soo);    // print 101
    System.out.println(this.soo);   // print 101
  }
}
```

The **super** variable refers to the superclass type of the current object within the scope of a nonstatic method. This example shows a typical usage of the *super* variable:

```
class Goo {
  int soo = 101;
  void test () {
    System.out.println(soo);    // print 101
    System.out.println(this.soo);   // print 101
  }
}
class Foo extends Goo {
  int too = 201;
  void play () {
    System.out.println(this.too);   // print 201
    System.out.println(super.soo); // print 101
  }
}
```

Methods

Methods of a class are the implemented functions and procedures that manipulate data. They are what do the work. Every operation on data you create must be implemented as a method. Methods can be declared in either an interface or a class, depending on the situation.

Syntax and Structure Methods defined in a class body must possess the following syntax and structure. (Keywords inside brackets are optional).

```
[comment] [modifiers] return_type method_name (parm, parm, ...) {
  ... method_body ...
}
```

Here is an example of a method declaration:

```
/* This method has a preceding comment used to generate documentation.
Notice the specialized comment form. This method has a modifier of
public, a return type of void, a method name of Render, and a comma-
separated parameter list followed by the method body or implementa-
tion. */
/** Method name Render of class Display */
public void Render (int x, int y, Graphics g) {
  if(x >= 0 && y <= 1000) {
    ... render graphic ...
  }
}
```

Methods must have a return type except for the specialized method **constructor**, which you will learn more about in the following section. A **void** return type of a nonconstructor method indicates that it returns no values; it just does some work. A method can have a parameter list with individual parameters separated by commas. Each parameter consists of a type and parameter name pair. A method's parameter list may also be empty. In the prior example, **int x** asserts that variable **x** is of type **int**.

Local variables of a method—those declared within the body of a method—cannot conflict with parameter variables. For instance, this Java code fragment is illegal because the **index** variable conflicts with the parameter-declared **index** variable. This causes a runtime error.

```
class Test {
  public void Display (int index) {
    int count = 0;
    /* errant redeclaration of index parameter variable */
    while (int index <= count) {
      ...
    }
  }
}
```

You can create a new method for a class with the same name as another method for the same class or its superclass. This is known as *polymorphism* and is used to overload and override class methods. Overriding means a different implementation, while overloading means providing a different interface to a method.

Overloading As an example of overloading, the Render method is overloaded three times in this Java code fragment:

```java
class Display {
  public void Render (int x, int y, Graphics g) {
    if(x >= 0 && y <= 1000) {
      ... render graphic ...
    }
  }
  public void Render (int x, int y, Image i) {
    if(x >= 0 && y <= 1000) {
      ... render graphic ...
    }
  }
  public void Render (int x, int y, int z, Graphics g) {
    if(x >= 0 && y <= 1000) {
      ... render graphic ...
    }
  }
}
```

You can call this Render method with three different parameter lists depending on your intentions or data set, as shown here:

```java
Graphics g;
Image i;
Display d;

d.Render(12,123,g);
d.Render(12,123,i);
d.Render(12,123,9,g);
```

Overload Resolution To call the correct overloaded method, a set of rules is needed. Remember, an overloaded method has the same name as another method for the same class, but differs in the elements found in its parameter list. This parameter list can vary by the number of parameters and the types assigned to those parameters.

The Java compiler incorporates a variety of built-in heuristics to resolve its choice of method with the lowest cost, where such cost is determined by the amount of conversion required for the compiler to switch between differing object types. The compiler considers for matches only those methods with the correct name and the correct number of parameters. After the compiler determines all costs, it picks the conversion with the lowest cost. Some conversions incur high costs and may result in data loss; these are called nonisomorphic conversions. If more than one conversion has the same lowest cost, the match is considered to be ambiguous and a compile-time error occurs.

Overriding You can override a method's implementation by declaring a new method with the same name found in the original superclass, with the same **return** type, and with the same parameter list. The only difference lies in the internals of the method's implementation. This might be done to increase performance of an implemented algorithm.

You simply call the new method in the normal way, which automatically implements the new algorithm. To invoke the original method of the superclass, you use the **super** variable. Here's an example:

```
fence_sort();        /* use new overriding implementation */
super.fence_sort(); /* invoke overridden implementation */
```

Local Variables for Methods A local variable for a method is a variable declared within the scope of the method. Before a local variable is used, it must be declared and initialized. Failure to declare and initialize a local variable before it is used results in a compile-time error. For example, in this Java code fragment, the local variable **point** is declared within a method named Render:

```
public void Render (int x, int y) {
   int point = 0; // local variable of Render method
   ... method body ...
}
```

Constructors

A **constructor** is a specialized method for a class, the function of which is to initialize an object. **Constructors** have the same name as the class they initialize, but don't have a return type. Specifying a return type results in a compile-time error. **Constructors** are magically called by the system upon the creation of an object by instantiating a class and they cannot be called explicitly by sending a message to an object. You can declare **constructors** as **public**, which allows objects of this type to be instantiated outside their package's scope.

You can overload **constructors** in the same manner as methods. This allows you to create variants of an object without creating a separate class for each object. These variants may differ slightly.

You must remember three things when using **constructors**:

1. Instance variables of a method cannot be referenced before an object is constructed. The **constructor** must be called first.
2. Instance variables of a superclass are initialized by:
    *   a **constructor** of the current class;
    *   the immediate superclass **constructor**; or
    *   if neither of these applies, the superclass **constructor** without parameters is invoked.
3. **Constructors**—either superclass or same class—called within a **constructor** must be the first code within the **constructor** body.

Here are examples:

```
// invoke constructor of immediate superclass
class AA extends A {
  char c;
  AA (int x) {
    // call immediate superclass constructor
    super(char c);
  }
}
// invoke constructor of current class
class AA extends A {
  int a;
  // constructor 1
  AA (int x) {
    ... constructor body ...
  }
  // constructor 2
  AA (float y) {
    // call matching constructor in current class
    this(int a); // calls constructor 1
  }
}
```

47

If you don't declare a constructor, the compiler automatically generates one for the class in the form:

```
class AA extends A {
  // automatically generated constructor
  AA () {
    super();
  }
}
```

Creating an Object with the *new* Operator

To instantiate a class (a template describing the behavior and state of an object) as an object (an instance of a class) you use the **new** operator. This explicitly allocates storage for the object. All objects are allocated from the memory heap.

Garbage collection is performed periodically on this heap to relieve the programmer from the rigors of memory management. When using Java, programmers need not explicitly allocate and deallocate storage for objects. The garbage collection service never deallocates storage that remains referenced, nor that which results in a dangling pointer. This alleviates the memory leak problem common to many C and C++ applications.

The **new** operator performs three tasks:

1. it allocates memory from the heap;
2. it initializes any class instance variables; and
3. it calls the appropriate **constructor**.

Syntax and Structure To create an object from a class template, use the **new** operator, passing the parameters for its **constructor** in this way:

```
variable = new ClassName(parm, parm,...);
```

Here are two examples:

```
Date d = new Date(); /* assign current system time to variable d */
String s = new d.toString(); /* call toString method of Date class */
```

An object can have the value of **null**. The **null** keyword means that an object currently has no viable instances. It can be used in the same places you would expect to use an object. It can also be cast to any class type.

Static Variables, Initializers, and Methods

A class method or variable can be declared as **static**. The **static** keyword indicates that a variable or a method of a class applies to the class itself and not to instances of that class—that is, not to instantiated objects. This means that a **static** variable's value cannot be altered by an instance of the class. These variables can have typical initializers, just like those of instance variables.

A **static** variable for a class exists only once per class regardless of how many instances currently exist. Finally, you can access a **static** variable through the name of the class or through an instance of a class, as will be demonstrated later. Here's an example:

```
class AA {
  int a;  // instance variable
  static aa;  // static variable
  AA () {
    ... constructor body ...
  }
    ... method bodies ...
}
```

A block of code can also be declared as **static**. This is called a static initializer. Here's an example:

```
class AA {
  int a;  // instance variable
  static int A[] = new int[10];
  /* static initializer; block of code marked as static */
  static {
    for (int index; index < 10; index++) {
      A[index] = 0; // initialize static array A
    }
  }
  AA () {
    ... constructor body ...
  }
    ... method bodies ...
}
```

Static methods must not reference class instance variables. Static methods are required to use only static variables and methods. Static methods are accessed through the name of the class or through an instance of a class. Here is an example:

```
class AA {
  int a;  // instance variable
  static aa;  // static variable
  static int A[] = new int[10];
  /* static initializer; block of code marked as static */
  static {
    for (int index; index < 10; index++) {
      A[index] = 0; // initialize static array A
    }
  }
  AA () {
    ... constructor body ...
  }
  // instance method One
  void One (int x) {
    this.x = x;
  }
  // static method Two
  static void Two (int xx) {
    AA.aa = xx;
  }
  // static method Three
  static void Three () {
    AA z = new AA();  /* call constructor for this class */
    AA.aa = 145; /* valid: aa is a static variable of class */
    AA.Two(123); /* valid: Two is a static method of class */
    z.aa = 1;    /* valid: aa is static instance variable */
    z.Two(44);   /* valid: Two is a static method of instance */
    z.i = 5;     /* valid: i is an instance variable of instance */
    AA.a = 2;    /* invalid: a instance var is not static */
    AA.One(9);   /* invalid: One is not a static method */
  }
}
```

For **static** methods and variables, the order in which classes and their associated methods and instance variables are declared is immaterial. You may, however, experience initialization problems stemming from cyclic referencing. Initializations occur in lexical order—that is, in the order tokens enter the data stream. Forward referencing by the methods for other object methods and instance variables is permitted.

Access Specifiers

Java provides three access specifiers for methods and variables. They are the keywords **protected**, **private**, and **public**. They allow a programmer to control access to methods, constructors, and class variables. Any class, method, or variable designated as **public** is accessible by any system object. If they are marked as **private**, they are accessible only within their declared classes. They are considered **final** and cannot be overridden by any subclasses.

A compile-time error occurs if you try to override a **private** method or variable from a subclass, or if you try to assign **private** access to a **public** or **protected** method or variable. If a method or variable is marked as **protected**, it is only accessible by subclasses and the class in which it is declared. Sibling classes are denied access to **protected** methods or variables. Finally, classes, methods, or variables that are not designated as either **public** or **private** are accessible only within the scope of their packages.

Variable Scope Rules

When you create a new class by subclassing an existing class, any declarations within the existing class are visible in the subclass within the scope of the new class' package. Within a method, certain scope rules are in effect when you reference a variable. They are presented in order here:

1. The local scope is searched, including successive blocks within a method.
2. The class scope is searched by first examining the current class variables; if they don't exist, the superclass variables are examined, continuing through superclasses and terminating in the **Object** class. Imported classes and packages are then searched. If this search is fruitless, a compile-time error occurs.

Finally, as you would expect, variables with the same name within the same class are not allowed and result in a compile-time errors.

Interfaces

An interface is a collection of prototypes of each class method providing encapsulation of method protocols. The implementations of these protocols are not restricted to any particular inheritance hierarchy that provides flexibility. Excluding abstract classes—classes declared for common methods and variables but never instantiated—a class must implement all methods of its interface.

An interface is declared with the keyword **interface**. Similar to classes, interfaces are either **private** by default or **public**. The methods of an interface are always public and abstract, and are implemented as:

```
return_type method_name (parm, parm, ...);
```

Variables of an interface are **public**, **static**, or **final** and cannot include modifiers; they must be initialized. Variables of an interface are specified as follows.

```
variable_type variable_name;
```

Here's a valid interface declaration:

```
public Interface Goo {
    // interface variables
    static final int one = 1;
    static final int two = 2;
    static final into three = 3;
    // interface methods
    public abstract int methodOne(int i);
    public abstract int methodTwo(char c);
}

public class Too implements Goo {
    ...
    int methodOne (int i) {
        ...
    }
    int methodTwo (char c){
    ...
    }
}
```

Interfaces Used as Types

Using an interface as a type in Java relieves the programmer from constructing abstract (mix-in) superclasses to share commonalities, which is a common practice in C++. It also allows the programmer to specify a particular interface to be implemented by an object. Here's an example of using an interface as a type:

```
public class Too {
  int i;  // instance variable
  /* method using the Goo interface type in a parameter list */
  void example (Goo g) {
    g.methodOne(4);   // use Goo interface method
    g.methodTwo('a'); // use Goo interface method
  }
}
```

Combining Interfaces

You can combine interfaces from more than one class. Here's an example of the Goo interface extending the Soo and Roo interfaces:

```
public interface Goo extends Soo, Roo {
  ... interface body ...
}
```

This allows you to extend and specialize your interfaces to new classes.

Packages

A **package** is a collection of classes and interfaces that is used for their management. A **package** is an abstract name for a collection of classes and interfaces that is used to avoid or resolve class, method, or variable name contentions. Every class and interface is contained in a **package**.

Package Specification

A Java package is specified by the keyword **package**. The package name is specified as a list of words separated by a period, with the initial name in the list indicating the class owner and developer. The **package** declaration must be the first statement other than comments and whitespace in a compilation unit. For example, the following Java source code fragment declares two packages:

```
// declare a simple package
package myPackage;
// declare a more complex package
package myPackage.myOtherStuff.myLastStuff;
```

When you define a compilation unit—a collection of classes and interfaces—without a package statement, the unit is designated as the default package with no name. In this case, you could not import this unit to other classes without declaring it as a package.

Using Another Package's Classes and Interfaces

The OO paradigm's power and expressiveness include the capability to reuse existing classes and interfaces. Java provides such a mechanism, which allows you to make classes and interfaces available across package boundaries.

The **import** keyword asserts that external classes and interfaces are imported into the current package. By default, a compilation unit automatically imports all classes and interfaces contained in its own package. Here's an example that imports all public classes of the user-defined MarkUp package:

```
// import all classes from MarkUp
import MarkUp.*;
```

The asterisk says to import all public classes of the package.

You can specify classes or interfaces from an external package in two ways: by importing the package, classes, and interfaces into the current name space; or by prefacing each reference to an external class or interface with a package statement. Here's an example of each approach:

```
/* Importing all external classes and interfaces of myPackage */
import myPackage.*;
/* prefacing with package statement */
myPackage.myClass item = new myPackage.myClass();
```

Finally, specifying an ambiguous class or interface name, thereby causing name space collisions within the current package, results in a compile-time error. You can avoid this by qualifying the class or interface name with the full package name.

Expressions

Java expressions are very similar to expressions in C and C++. In this section, you learn about valid operations found in expressions, and about Java's cast and conversion mechanisms.

Operators

Java has unary and binary operators. A unary operator acts on a single operand, whereas a binary operator works on two operands. Multiple operators may occur within an expression. To guarantee that an expression resolves to the same answer each time, Java imposes a precedence order for operators.

Table 2-4 presents a list of operators specified by precedence from highest to lowest. Highest means that the operation will done before another operation with lower precedence. Operators of the same precedence are done in lexical order—how they appear in the data stream, which moves from right to left in an expression.

Table 2-4: Precedence Order of Java Operators, from Highest to Lowest

```
. [] ()
++ — ! ~ instanceof
* / %
+ -
<< >> >>>
< > <= >=
== !=
&
^
|
&&
||
?:
= += -= *= /= &= |= ^= %= >>= <<= >>>=

'
```

Integers Operations on integers depend on the type of integer operands involved. But no matter what types of integer operands are involved, the results or an operation will be **int** or **long**, never **byte**, **short**, or **char**.

If both operands are **int**, the result of the operation is also an **int**. If one operand is **int** and the other is **long**, the result is **long**. Finally, if a result is outside the boundary of the result type, the result of the operation is reduced by the integer modulo function of the range of the result type. For example, if the result of adding two 8-bit integers results in an integer larger than 65,536, the number is reduced by truncating the excess significant bits. Table 2-5 summarizes these integer operators.

Table 2-5: Integer Operators in Java

TYPE	OPERATOR	OPERATION	NOTES
Unary	-	negation	
	~	bitwise complement	
	++	increment	postfix and prefix
	—	decrement	postfix and prefix
	abs()	absolute value	usage: a = abs(3);
Binary	+	addition	
	+=	addition	(a = a + b) == (a += b)
	-	subtraction	
	-=	subtraction	(a = a - b) == (a -= b)
	*	multiplication	
	*=	multiplication	(a = a * b) == (a *= b)
	/	division	rounds toward zero; division by zero raises ArithimeticExpression;
	/=	division	(a = a / b) == (a /= b)
	%	modulo	%0 raises ArithimeticExpression
	%=	modulo	(a = a % b) == (a %= b)
	>>=	right shift (propogate sign)	(a = a >> b) == (a >>= b)
	<<	left shift	
	>>	right shift	sign is propagated
	>>>	zero-fill right shift	pads with zeros on left
	max()	maximum value of range	usage: i = max(x,y);
	min()	minimum value of range	usage: l = min(x,y);

Booleans Operations which take Boolean operands result in Boolean values, which may be either **true** or **false**. Table 2-6 summarizes the various Java Boolean operators.

Table 2-6: Boolean Operators in Java

Type	Operator	Operation	Notes
unary	!	negation	
binary	&	logical AND	evaluate both operands
	&=	logical AND	(a = a & b) == (a &= b)
	|	logical OR	evaluate both operands
	|=	logical OR	(a = a | b) == (a |= b)
	^	logical XOR	evaluate both operands
	^=	logical XOR	(a = a ^ b) == (a ^= b)
	&&	logical AND	shortcut evaluation of operands
	||	logical OR	shortcut evaluation of operands
	>	greater than	
	<	less than	
	>=	greater than or equal	
	<=	less than or equal	
	==	equality	
	!=	inequality	
ternary	?:	if, then	(if a then b) == (a?:b)

Floating-Point Numbers Operations on floating-point operands are similar to integer operations. Single-precision, floating-point expressions—each operand is a single-precision, floating-point value—produce single-precision results. If either operand is a double-precision type, double-precision operations are employed on the operands, resulting in a double-precision result.

Java does not have an ArithmeticException for floating-point values, but instead uses the IEEE 754 floating-point specification's NaN and Inf. For example, instead of an arithmetic exception being thrown on floating-point division by zero, Java returns Inf as the result. On the other hand, an error message is produced for an integer division by zero, because this is an invalid mathematical operation.

Operators for integer values behave the same as for floating-point numbers, with a couple of exceptions. The ++ and -- operators used with a floating-point operand result in adding 1.0 to the value. The modulo function (%) for floating-point values results in the remainder value—that is, what's left over after a division operation—typed as a floating-point value. Finally, be careful when checking equality between floating-point values. This is a common warning for all programming languages because floating-point values are dependent on their formats. This presents an ordering problem. It cannot guarantee that if "a < b" is true, then "b >= a" is also true. This stems from the NaN and Inf values of the IEEE 754 specification.

Arrays Operations on Java arrays return the value of an element of the array. Such operations have the following syntax:

```
array-variable [expression]
```

The value that results from the expression within the brackets must be within a range of values from 0 to the length of the array minus 1. These boundary checks are performed at run time by the Java interpreter. Here are some valid examples of such references:

```
int I = new int[5];
int a.length;
int b = 2;
int c = 1;
a = I[1]; // get second element
b = I[b+c]; // get fourth element
length = I.length(); // get length of array
a = I[length - 1]; // get last element
```

Strings Operations on strings are really operations on **String** objects. The + operator concatenates two **String** objects. If either of the operands in the operation is not of the **String** class type, it is automatically converted. The += operator also produces concatenated **String** objects. Here are examples:

```
int I = 12;
String S = "abc = ";
System.out.println("I has a value of: " + I + "\n");
String echo_s = "I has a value of: " + I + "\n";
S += I; /* I is converted to String before concatenation */
System.out.println(S); // prints "abc = 12"
```

Objects Java provides an **instanceof** binary operator for an object—that is, an instance of a class. Java tests if the current object is an instance of the operand that is a class or subclass. For example:

```
if ( currentObject instanceof myObject ) {
  ... do something ...
}
```

Conversions and Casts

One of Java's most noteworthy security features is the restriction of runtime casting and conversion of objects and variables. This prevents the possibility of malicious corruption of your system. Here is a summary of allowable casts and conversions:

- Objects may not be cast to base types such as **Object**.
- Floating-point and integer numbers can be cast back and forth.
- Integers cannot be cast to objects or arrays.
- An instance of a class can be cast to a superclass.
- An instance of a class can be cast to a subclass with a runtime check to ensure that it is a valid instance of the subclass or one of its subclasses. A ClassCastException is raised if the instance isn't a valid subclass or sub-subclass.

All other casting operations are illegal and cause compile-time errors.

Statements

In this section you learn about the type and placement of Java statements in source code. These include declarations, expressions, control flow, and exception statements.

Declarations

A Java declaration may occur in the source code wherever a statement is allowed. Declarations have a scope that is determined by the enveloping block. Declarations can also occur within **for** statements, such as:

```
for (int index = 0; index < 10; index++) {
  ... body of for loop ...
}
```

The scope of the index variable in the above example is within the **for** loop. After the **for** loop terminates, the index variable is out of scope.

Expressions

Expressions are statements within Java source code and are evaluated accordingly. Here are examples:

```
flag = true;
a += b;
myObject.myMethod(123);
```

Control Flow

Logical flow within Java source code is expressed using control statements. The following is a summary of these statements taken from the Java language specification. Optional items are enclosed within brackets.

```
if (boolean) statement;
else statement;

switch (expression) {
  case expression: statements;
  default: statements;
}

break [label];
continue [label];
return expression;
for([expression]; [expression]; [expression]) statement;
while(boolean) statement;
do statement while(boolean);
label: statement;
```

Java supports labeled blocks of code and labeled breaks out of code blocks. The following rules govern such labeling:

- Any statement in source code can have a label.

- If a **continue** statement has a label, it must have the same label as its enveloping loop.

- If a **break** statement has a label, it must have the same label as its enveloping statement.

Exceptions

Java provides a set of exceptions it raises when errors occur within a program. The default action upon the raising of an exception is to print an error message to STDOUT and terminate the current execution thread. Exception-handling services are provided by the Java runtime system.

Classes can also define their own exceptions with the **throw** keyword. Under appropriate conditions, this causes an exception to be thrown, which in turn causes execution to switch to the appropriate exception handler. These handlers are derived from the **Exception** system class. For example:

```
class newException extends Exception {
    ... body of class ...
}
class Foo {
  void trap () {
    if(error trapped) {
      throw new newException();
    }
  }
}
```

You can implement an exception handler of your own to trap the exception and take the appropriate action. These can be nested if necessary. To write an exception handler, you must use the **try** keyword combined with one or more **catch** keywords. The code that might raise an exception is enveloped by a **try**. Each exception has its own **catch** statement, which takes either a class or an interface as a parameter. Here's an example:

```
try {
  ptr.value = 13;
}
catch (Exception e) { System.out.println("undetermined error"); }
catch (Object o) { System.out.println("object exception trapped"); }
catch (NullPointerException npe) { System.out.println("null ptr"); }
```

The correct **catch** is determined by matching the exception parameter with the same class type or superclass type, or the interface, which is then implemented by the exception class.

finally The **finally** keyword specifies that a statement guarantees a block of code will be executed regardless of whether an exception was raised or not. For example, the **finally** statement will be executed in the following code even if a **continue**, **break**, **return**, or **throw** statement is executed:

```
try {
  ptr.value = 134;
}
finally {
  System.out.println("Ptr = " + ptr.value);
}
```

Runtime Exceptions The Java runtime system provides a set of exceptions to handle runtime errors. These are classified as arithmetic, null pointer, class, array, memory, type, link, and internal exceptions. Table 2-7 summarizes the Java runtime exceptions.

Table 2-7: Runtime Exceptions in Java

EXCEPTION NAME	CAUSE OF RAISING EXCEPTION
ArithmeticException	integer division by zero, or integer modulus by zero
NullPointerException	attempt to access method or variable in a null array or object
IncompatibleClassChangeException	attempt to change class definition without recompiling other referencing classes
ClassCastException	attempt to cast object to a class when the object is not a valid instance of the type's class or subclass
NegativeArraySizeException	attempt to create negative length of array
OutofMemoryException	attempt to create a new object when sufficient memory is unavailable
NoClassDefFoundException	attempt to reference an undefined class
IncompatibleTypeException	attempt to instantiate an interface

Table 2-7: *Continued*

EXCEPTION NAME	CAUSE OF RAISING EXCEPTION
ArrayIndexOutOfBoundsException	attempt to access an element outside the boundaries of the array
UnsatisfiedLinkException	attempt to link a native method that cannot be linked
InternalException	the run-time system failed

Summary

By design, Java's syntax, concepts, and general statements are quite similar to C and C++. In Java, however, the following observations apply:

- Floating-point types are implemented in a machine-independent way.
- Character arrays are instances of the **String** object.
- Classes are instantiated with the **new** operator, which allocates storage on the heap.
- Garbage collection services provided by the Java system alleviate memory leaks and dangling pointers.
- Java has no pointer arithmetic.
- An interface allows public access to the methods of the class that implements it.
- A package describes a collection of classes and interfaces.

Expressions and statements in Java are derived explicitly from C and C++. Finally, the Java runtime system provides a set of exceptions to handle runtime errors in your programs. All in all, Java offers the power and flexibility of C and C++, but includes more rigorous built-in typing, casting, and error-handling mechanisms.

In the next chapter, we take all this explanation about Java's objects, methods, operators, and exceptions and put it to work as you explore the ins and outs of programming Java applets. This will be your ticket to writing your own Java code, so it's the most important introduction we'll make in the entire book.

## CHAPTER 3

Writing a
Java Applet

hen a HotJava <APP> tag is embedded in an HTML document, it can augment that document's content with additional functionality. In fact, an applet can bring such a document to life. Although this new HTML tag is currently a third-party extension (proposed and defined by Sun Microsystems), it provides a mechanism to augment a document's content and its presentation.

Since the HotJava browser can execute Java applets, it is more flexible than other WWW browsers. The HotJava browser can therefore deliver many new types of information to users without requiring the installation or deployment of new helper applications. It's a way to open the door to new types of data and information without requiring changes to the software and configuration information that Web servers use to handle Web services.

In this chapter, you learn how to design and code a simple Java applet. You also learn about the basic structure of a Java applet, and how to create and save such an applet. Finally, we walk you through the step-by-step creation of an example Java applet, DocFooter, which provides a document footer positioned at the end of any HTML document in which it is invoked. But before we start, you also need to understand what's required to use Java and to make Java applets (or applications) run.

Java Runtime Requirements

A Java applet is nothing more than a text file with a .java extension. This extension supplies a cue to the user that the file contains Java source code. It is also a clue to the Java source code compiler, **javac**. The result of successful compilation is a file with a .class extension. This binary file contains Java bytecode. A .class file is not human readable, but you can access it with the class disassembler, **javap**.

In this chapter, we create a Java applet called DocFooter.java and a Java executable class called DocFooter.class. To launch this applet from within an HTML document, you use the following HTML statement.

```
<APP CLASS="DocFooter">
```

Here's a summary of the relationship between a Java applet and its .class file:

- DocFooter.java—Java applet source code file
- DocFooter.class—bytecode compiled Java class
- <APP CLASS="DocFooter">—HTML tag specification

The Java runtime system imposes strict requirements on where applets are created and compiled. The Java source code file and resulting compiled class binary must reside in the same directory. For the purpose of our example in this chapter, we assume the following directory structure:

- /html—contains .html documents
- /html/images—contains .gif image files
- /html/audio—contains .au audio files
- /html/classes—contains .java and .class files

In addition, here are the pertinent environment variables and their values for our example Java applet. These variables control system file access for the HotJava browser and the Java runtime system.

```
setenv CLASSPATH .:/html/classes
setenv HOTJAVA_HOME /export/home/hotjava/
setenv HOTJAVA_READ_PATH .:/html
setenv HOTJAVA_WRITE_PATH /tmp/:/devices/:/dev/:~/.hotjava/
```

Applet Variables, Constructors, and Methods

Before we proceed, we need to introduce the variables, constructors, and methods in the browser.Applet base class. In the following three sections, you learn more about these variables, constructors, and methods as we explore the Java Applet class. You need to reference this information when building your own applets.

Applet Instance Variables

- appletURL—URL for the applet

```
public URL appletURL
```

- documentURL—URL for the document containing the applet

```
public URL documentURL
```

- bgColor—background color for the applet

```
public Color bgColor
```

- fgColor—foreground color for the applet

```
public Color fgColor
```

- font—font for the applet

```
public Font font
```

- height—height for the applet window in pixels

```
public int height
```

- width—width for applet window in pixels

```
public int width
```

- item—name of the AppletDisplayItem canvas that displays the applet

```
public AppletDisplayItem item
```

- tag—associated HTML <APP> tag that invokes the applet

```
public TagRef tag
```

Applet Constructor

- Applet( )—creates an instance of the Java Applet class (required to run any Java applet)

```
public Applet()
```

Applet Instance Methods

- destroy()—cleans up resources after killing an applet (called implicitly by HotJava when an applet is exited)

```
protected void destroy()
```

- getAttribute(String)—gets a specific attribute from the <APP> tag specification in an HTML document

```
public String getAttribute (String name)
```

- getAudioData(String)—gets the AudioData object associated with String name, which contains an audio data reference passed into the program as an input parameter

```
public AudioData getAudioData(String name)
```

- getAudioData(URL)—gets an AudioData object containing audio data given a URL that points to the location of an .au (audio) file

```
public AudioData getAudioData(URL url)
```

- getAudioStream(URL)—gets a stream of audio data specified by a URL

```
public InputStream getAudioStream(URL url)
```

- getColor(int,int,int)—gets a Red/Green/Blue (RGB) color triplet

```
public Color getColor(int r, int g, int b)
```

- getContinuousAudioStream(URL)—gets a continuous stream of audio data as specified by the URL

```
public InputStream getContinuousAudioStream(URL url)
```

- getFocus()—gets the focus for the applet

```
public void getFocus()
```

- getFont(String,int)—gets a font with a specific name (String) and size (int)

```
public Font getFont(String name, int size)
```

- getFont(String,int,int)—gets a font with a specific name, style, and size

```
public Font getFont(String name, int style, int size)
```

- getImage(String)—gets an image from the specified file name

```
public Image getImage(String name)
```

- getImage(URL)—gets the image specified by the URL

```
public Image getImage(URL url)
```

- gotFocus( )—signals that the focus was acquired, and input into the applet can now be accepted

```
public void gotFocus()
```

- init( )—initializes the applet (called automatically)

```
protected void init()
```

- isActive( )—signals if the applet is active in current HTML document

```
public boolean isActive()
```

- keyDown(int)—the character corresponding to a depressed key is rendered in the applet and the key retains the focus

```
public void keyDown(int key)
```

- lostFocus( )—the applet lost the focus

```
public void lostFocus()
```

- mouseDown(int,int)—if a mouse button is depressed while the pointer is at (x,y) pixel of display relative to the upper-left corner of the applet (0,0), the (x,y) values are passed as parameters to this method

```
public void mouseDown(int x, int y)
```

- mouseDrag(int,int)—if the mouse pointer is moved while mouse button is depressed at (x,y) pixel of display relative to the upper-left corner of the applet, (0,0), the most recent (x,y) values are passed as parameters to this method

```
public void mouseDrag(int x, int y)
```

- mouseEnter( )—called when the mouse enters applet regardless of mouse button state

```
public void mouseEnter()
```

- mouseExit( )—called when mouse exits applet regardless of mouse button state

```
public void mouseExit()
```

- mouseMove(int,int)—mouse pointer is moved with mouse button to (x,y) pixel of display relative to the upper-left corner of the applet (0,0)

```
public void mouseMove(int x, int y)
```

- mouseUp(int,int)—mouse button released while pointer at (x,y) pixel of display relative to the upper-left corner of the applet (0,0)

```
public void mouseUp(int x, int y)
```

- paint(Graphics)—paints the applet on the AppletDisplayItem canvas

```
public void paint(Graphics g)
```

- play(String)—plays an audio sample—data obtained using getAudioData from the value supplied by String name (provides shortcut method for playing audio)

```
public void play(String name)
```

- play(AudioData)—plays an audio clip specified by AudioData, which contains a stream of audio data

```
public void play(AudioData data)
```

- repaint( )—repaints the applet's display

```
public void repaint()
```

- resize(int,int)—resizes the AppletDisplayItem canvas to display the applet

```
public void resize(int width, int height)
```

- showDocument(URL)—displays the document specified by URL

```
public void showDocument(URL doc)
```

- showStatus(String)—displays status information as a string at the bottom of the HotJava display window

```
public void showStatus(String msg)
```

- start( )—called by HotJava to start the applet

```
protected void start()
```

- startPlaying(InputStream)—starts playing stream of audio data

```
public void startPlaying(InputStream stream)
```

- stop( )—called by HotJava to stop the execution of an applet

```
protected void stop()
```

- stopPlaying(InputStream)—stops playing stream of audio data

```
public void stopPlaying(InputStream stream)
```

- update(Graphic)—updates graphic on AppletDisplayItem canvas

```
public void update(Graphics g)
```

Java Applet Structure

In this section, you learn about the specific structure of a Java applet. An applet is a subclass of the base system class, Applet, in the browser system package. Java's browser.Applet is a subclass of the most basic system class, java.lang.Object, which is the mother of all classes in the Java programming environment.

An applet, such as the DocFooter applet that we create in this chapter, is an extension or specialization of the base Applet class. Here's a specification for the basic structure of the DocFooter applet:

```
import browser.Applet; /* import the system base class Applet */

class DocFooter extends Applet {
    ... body of class ...
}
```

Notice that the name of the class, DocFooter, is the same as the value of the CLASS attribute of the <APP> tag:

```
<APP CLASS="DocFooter">
```

Once an applet is loaded by the Java runtime system, it is associated with a system class called AppletDisplayItem in the browser system package. This class is a container that contains the applet's information, which is rendered by the HotJava browser. This class is an extension of the DisplayItem class of the **awt** (abstract windowing toolkit) system package, which contains windowing-specific interfaces and classes.

An applet must contain four important methods that are invoked by the HotJava browser: **init**, **start**, **stop**, and **destroy**. These four methods are implicitly called by the HotJava browser, so you do not need to call them directly; you just define them.

These four methods are specified in this example:

```
import browser.Applet; /* import the system base class Applet */

class DocFooter extends Applet {
  protected void init() {
    ... body of method ...
  }
  protected void start() {
    ... body of method ...
  }
  protected void stop() {
    ... body of method ...
  }
  protected void destroy() {
    ... body of method ...
  }
}
```

init()

The init( ) method belonging to the Applet class is invoked after the applet has been loaded into memory by the Java runtime system. In this method, you can code tasks to initialize instance variables, resize the AppletDisplayItem, import or include any resources, or set text properties for objects, such as font and color.

Here's a simple specification of the init( ) method:

```
protected void init () {
  resize(400,100); /* set width and height of the AppletDisplayItem */
  logo = getImage("images/logo.gif"); /* retrieve .GIF image */
}
```

This example code resizes the Applet's canvas area in the HotJava browser to 400 pixels wide by 100 pixels high. The resize method is implemented in the browser.Applet base class. The init( ) method also retrieves a .gif image from the file system. The code instructs the runtime system to retrieve a file named logo.gif in the images directory, specified

relative to the current HTML document. You can also specify a URL
rather than a file as a parameter to the getImage method for the
browser.Applet class.

start()

The start( ) protected method belonging to the Applet class is invoked
by the HotJava browser every time the applet's HTML document is
loaded successfully. This method provides a method for the applet to
launch background threads such as playing a looped animation or playing an audio sound bite upon start-up.

Here's a sample specification for start( ):

```
protected void start() {
  getFocus(); // get window focus
}
```

The above example gets the current window focus once the applet's
HTML document is rendered by HotJava.

stop()

The stop( ) protected method is invoked by the HotJava browser immediately after the applet's HTML document is removed from the HotJava
display window. This method terminates any executing threads
spawned by or belonging to the applet. This method is guaranteed to
be called prior to the execution of destroy( ) as a part of the standard
sequence of terminating a Java applet.

Here's a sample specification for this method:

```
protected void stop() {
  audioThread = null; // terminate an audio clip
}
```

This example terminates any audio clip that might still be playing
once the applet's HTML document has been removed from the HotJava
display window.

destroy()

The destroy( ) protected method is executed by the HotJava browser
to remove the applet from memory, which completely terminates its

execution. If the applet is still active, stop() will be called prior to calling destroy(). Here's a sample destroy() specification:

```
protected void destroy() {
   closedB(); /* close an open database with an instance method */
}
```

This example calls an instance method defined in the subclass that closes any open database and commits any pending updates before terminating execution of the applet. The destroy() method lets applets terminate gracefully, without leaving data in an uncertain or incorrect state, and ensures that the applet's resources are released.

Creating Your First Java Applet

In this section, we guide you through the step-by-step creation of a Java applet called DocFooter.java. Before implementing the DocFooter applet, you need to determine the problem to be solved and the system resources the solution requires.

DocFooter Applet Design

The DocFooter applet provides a dynamically-created footer that can be appended to an HTML document. Of course, the HTML code <APP CLASS="DocFooter"> must be embedded within the HTML document to include this applet. You also must provide values for the input variables to the DocFooter applet, e.g., EMAIL="name@address".

What the DocFooter applet does is append a byline to an HTML document. A document footer should contain information about the HTML document, including the author's name, when it was last updated, and whom to contact if a problem is encountered. Table 3-1 suggests information that might be included in a document footer.

Table 3-1: Suggestions for Document Footer Information

Author's name	Author's organization	Author's phone number	Author's e-mail address
Author's postal address	Document owner's name	Document owner's e-mail address	Document owner's postal address

Table 3-1: *Continued*

Legal disclaimer	Date of document's last update	Organization's logo	Copyright notice
URL of the document	Navigational links		

In our DocFooter applet, the document footer that the applet creates and appends to the current HTML document presents the following information:

- Company logo
- Date last updated
- Author's e-mail address
- Copyright notice
- URL of current document

Here's what it looks like:

Thu Aug 31 15:38:01 CDT 1995 by markg@hal.com
Copyright 1995. The Gaither Group. All rights reserved.
file:///u/markg/html/DocFooter.html

Figure 3-1: Example of information rendered by the DocFooter applet

Now that we have identified the information to be rendered by the DocFooter applet, we need to identify the system resources required to create an instance of a document footer.

The company logo is a GIF image file. Its absolute path is /html/images/logo.gif. The /html/image directory is part of the HOTJAVA_READ_PATH environment variable because it is a subdirectory of the /html directory. Recall, this variable's value was set to:

```
setenv HOTJAVA_READ_PATH .:/html
```

This specification includes all subdirectories of /html, including /html/images. Therefore, the Java runtime system has permission to read our logo image file, /html/images/logo.gif. Now that we have all the necessary system resources in place, it's time to start writing some Java code!

Step 1: Create DocFooter.java and Insert import Declarations

Change to the /html/classes directory and create a file named DocFooter.java using your favorite text editor. Then, determine which system level packages you need to complete the document footer. For our DocFooter applet, you need the following system packages:

- browser—contains all variables, constructors, and methods for the Applet class
- awt—provides interfaces and classes for rendering a graphics context in an AppletDisplayItem object
- net.www.html—provides interfaces, classes, and exceptions for manipulating HTML tags within an HTML document

Therefore, add these import statements into your Java source code file with your editor:

```
import browser.*; /* import all items of browser system package */
import awt.*; /* import all items of awt system package */
import net.www.html.*; /* import all items of net.www.html package */
```

Step 2: Insert class Declaration

In this step you insert the DocFooter class declaration. This indicates which system class is the superclass for your DocFooter class. Add this with your editor:

```
public class DocFooter extends Applet {


}
```

This asserts that your new subclass name DocFooter is derived from or specializes a general system class named Applet. This step is necessary for each applet you write. This declaration also specifies that the DocFooter class is a public class, which allows any other class to utilize the new DocFooter class and its attendant functionality.

Step 3: Insert class Variables

In this step you declare some class instance variables and decide which variables will be visible to other classes (public), which variables will be visible only to subclasses derived from the DocFooter class (protected), and which variables will only be visible to instances of the DocFooter class.

These instance variable declarations are typically entered immediately after the class declaration, but they may declared anywhere in the class definition as long as they are declared before they're used. They must, however, appear outside any methods defined for the class.

Here's the specification for your instance variables:

```
// declaration of instance variables
String date; // date of last update
String email; // author's e-mail address
String copyright; // copyright blurb
Image logo; // .GIF image of company logo
```

Step 4: Define init() Method

In this step, you code the set of initialization actions required when the applet is loaded into memory prior to its execution. This code is inserted into the init( ) method, which is called by the HotJava browser prior to start up.

Here's the specification of the init( ) method for the DocFooter class:

```
/* method invoked by HotJava to initialize the applet */
protected void init() {
    resize(500,100); /* 500 pixels wide & 100 pixels high canvas */
    logo = getImage("images/logo.gif"); /* retrieve .GIF file */

    /* get applet attributes from <APP> tag */
    date = getAttribute("LAST_UPDATED");
    email = getAttribute("EMAIL");
    copyright = getAttribute("COPY_RIGHT_NOTICE");
}
```

In the init( ) method, three activities are completed during initialization of the applet.

1. The canvas into which the applet is rendered, AppletDisplayItem, is allocated its size of 500 pixels wide and 100 pixels high.

2. Next, the .GIF image file containing the company logo is retrieved from the file system. The path, images/logo.gif, is relative to the /html directory. Therefore, the absolute path to this .GIF image files is /html/images/logo.gif.

77

3. Finally, the attributes of the <APP> tag are retrieved and stored as String type.

Step 5: Define paint() method

In this step, you code the paint( ) method for the DocFooter class. This method is called by the HotJava browser to render data onto its canvas. It takes a graphics object as its parameter.

Here's the specification for the paint( ) method:

```
/* definition of the paint() method of the DocFooter class */
public void paint(Graphics g) {

  /* render the logo image in the canvas; originate image at upper-
left corner of canvas */
  g.drawImage(logo,0,0);

  /* render string data into the canvas at specific spots */
  g.drawString(date + " by ",100,15);
  g.drawString(email,290,15);
  g.drawString(copyright,100,35);

  /* get the URL of the document with the embedded <APP> tag */
  URL url = new URL(documentURL,"");

  /* convert the URL to a string of typical representation */
   String urlstring = url.toExternalForm();

  /* render the URL string to the canvas */
  g.drawString(urlstring,100,55);
}
```

This method defines how an applet is rendered onto the canvas located in the HTML document that invokes it.

The Whole Applet, in One Piece!

Here's a listing of the complete DocFooter applet specification:

```
import browser.*; /* import all items of browser system package */
import awt.*; /* import all items of awt system package */
```

```
import net.www.html.*; /* import items from html networking package */

public class DocFooter extends Applet {

  /* declaration of instance variables */
 String date; /* date of last update */
 String email; /* author's e-mail address */
 String copyright; /* copyright blurb */
 Image logo; /* .GIF image of company logo */
/* make sure your logo is no larger than 80x80 pixels; otherwise, you
must adjust the canvas size */

  /* method invoked by HotJava to initialize the applet */
  protected void init() {
    resize(500,100); /* 500 pixels wide & 100 pixels high canvas */
    logo = getImage("images/logo.gif"); /* retrieve .GIF file */

    /* get applet attributes from <APP> tag */
    date = getAttribute("LAST_UPDATED");
    email = getAttribute("EMAIL");
    copyright = getAttribute("COPY_RIGHT_NOTICE");
  }
  /* definition of the paint() method of the DocFooter class */
  public void paint(Graphics g) {

    /* render the logo image in the canvas; originate at upper-left
corner of canvas */
    g.drawImage(logo,0,0);

    /* render string data into the canvas at specific spots */
    g.drawString(date + " by " + email,100,15);
    g.drawString(copyright,100,35);

    /* get the URL of the document with the embedded <APP> tag */
    URL url = new URL(documentURL,"");
```

```
/* convert the URL to its non-URL-encoded form */
 String urlstring = url.toExternalForm();


/* render the URL string to the canvas */
 g.drawString(urlstring,100,55);
}
}
```

Step 6: Compile DocFooter.java

You now will compile the DocFooter.java file into the DocFooter.class binary file, which will be located in the /html/classes directory. This binary representation of the DocFooter class will be created by a successful compilation using the Java compiler, **javac**. To compile your first Java applet, enter the following on the command line. We assume you're working in a UNIX environment. (Note: *chevelle:/html/classes>* is your temporary UNIX prompt.)

```
chevelle:/html/classes>javac DocFooter.java
```

If your system can't find **javac**, check your path environment variable and ensure it includes a path to the HotJava installation directory and its binaries.

A successful compilation results in the creation of a file called DocFooter.class in the /html/classes directory. Therefore, the absolute file name for the bytecode is /html/classes/DocFooter.class. This is the binary executable that is invoked by HotJava when an <APP> tag referencing the DocFooter class in an HTML document is executed.

If your compilation is unsuccessful, the errors detected in your Java code will be displayed with explanations. To correct these errors, edit your Java code file and ensure that it exactly agrees with the above code. Then save the file and recompile. Repeat as needed until you're successful.

To load the .html file into the HotJava browser that contains the <APP> that calls the DocFooter applet, type the URL for the document into the Document URL: window and press Enter. Another method is to select File|Open and enter the document's URL. Either way, you're ready to view your work.

Summary

The first thing you should do when writing an applet is to decide which system packages to import. You then define the methods that the HotJava browser calls for your applet. In the example we use throughout this chapter, these are init( ), start( ), stop( ), destroy( ), and paint( ).

Not all of these methods are required in every case; what you actually define depends on the problem. init( ) and paint( ) are the most commonly defined methods when subclassing the Applet class.

Finally, you compile your Java code into a binary file containing byte-code. This binary file is created by the **javac** compiler and has a .class extension. The class is executed by the HotJava browser after an HTML document with an embedded <APP> tag, which references the compiled class, is loaded into a browser's display window.

Congratulations! You're now a Java author! In the next chapter, we change our focus to the HTML document side of the equation, and discuss the details of Sun's proposed <APP> tag used to invoke Java applets.

Section

Two

Java Applets vs. Applications

*h*ere in Section 2, the second tutorial includes Chapters 4 and 5 and covers how to work with Java applets while contrasting them with stand-alone Java applications. You'll get a sense of the major intended uses for Java, both as dynamic extensions to HTML documents and as full-featured, stand-alone networked applications with profound dynamic and extensible data-handling capabilities.

In Chapter 4, Adding an Applet to an HTML Document, you learn about the characteristics of Sun's HTML extension tag, <APP>, used to invoke Java applets from within HTML documents. You also learn about how HotJava invokes and runs applets as you make your way through a couple of examples. This chapter includes step-by-step instructions on how to install, test, and use such applets.

In Chapter 5, Extending Applets, you learn analytical techniques that help you decide whether to extend existing Java objects and classes, redefine them, or build new ones from scratch. Again, you'll explore examples, then follow step-by-step instructions on extending an applet, testing your work, and using the results.

## CHAPTER 4

Adding an Applet to an

HTML Document

*n*ow that you've written your first Java applet and created your first new Java class, DocFooter, you need to test your applet. Applets are invoked by HotJava from within an HTML document specified in the form of a new HTML element called the APP element.

In this chapter, you learn about the APP element and how to use its attribute list to control your Java applet's behavior. You also learn how HotJava invokes each individual applet embedded in an HTML document. To aid your understanding, we present simple examples of the APP element in use. Finally, you learn how to specify the APP element so you can execute the new DocFooter class.

The APP Element

To add a Java applet that has been compiled into bytecode into your HTML document, you utilize the new HTML element named APP. The APP element follows this general syntax:

```
<APP
   CLASS="class name"
   SRC="URL"
   ALIGN="alignment"
   HEIGHT="height in pixels"
   WIDTH="width in pixels"
   APPLET_SPECIFIC_ATTRIBUTES="values"
...>
```

Notice that the last attribute specified is called APPLET_SPECIFIC_ATTRIBUTES. These attributes may be used to customize the applet's behavior by the HTML document's author. They act like command-line variables and supply their respective values. Such variables are optional; they can appear as a single variable and value pair, or as a list of variables with their associated values.

Here are examples:

```
<APP
   CLASS="Marfa"
   TYPE="hotel"
   SIMULATION="real-time"
   PRESS="true"
>
```

The first example presents one required attribute from the Java core set known as CLASS, which specifies the applet's name, and three optional applet-specific attributes that supply runtime values to the applet when invoked.

```
<APP
   CLASS="Teammate"
   SRC="http://www.flagstaff.high.edu/classes/"
   ALIGN="center"
>
```

This specification example invokes the Teammate applet with two other standard attributes, SRC and ALIGN, which are discussed later in this chapter. Notice that there are no applet-specific attributes defined in this example.

The APP element of the HotJava Document Type Definition, an extension of the HTML 3.0 DTD, defines an applet in the following SGML DTD declaration:

```
<!-- This declares the APP element. It requires a start tag. The -->
<!-- end tag is not required. This singleton element also         -->
<!-- contains no content.                                         -->
<!ELEMENT APP -- O  EMPTY>
```

The preceding code is SGML markup. SGML uses the string "<!--" to begin a comment, and "-->" to end a comment. Thus, the first 3 lines of the preceding code are comments. SGML also uses "<!" to begin a declaration, and ">" to close one. Thus, the "<!ELEMENT APP ...>" line is a declaration; in fact, it specifies the syntax for the APP tag in HTML.

In this example, the <APP> tag is similar to a buoy floating in the flow of the document. This tag has no content per se. The real information about the APP element comes from its attribute list. An example of the APP element in an HTML document is:

```
<APP CLASS="DocFooter">
```

That's it. Notice that the APP element has no content, it only has attribution. This is similar to the IMG element in the HTML 2.0 DTD in that APP derives its syntax and semantics from a world outside that defined by the HTML DTD.

The APP element also incorporates a set of attributes that provide presentation control directives, the location of the applet's bytecode, and other applet-specific attributes. Here's the HotJava DTD specification for the attribute list for an APP element:

```
<!-- This is the list of attributes for the APP element. -->
<!ATTLIST APP
   class CDATA #REQUIRED
   src CDATA #IMPLIED
   align (bottom|top|middle) #IMPLIED
   width NUMBER #IMPLIED
   height NUMBER #IMPLIED
>
```

Let's look at each attribute in the APP element a bit closer. Also, remember that HTML tag names are not case sensitive so class and

87

CLASS attributes of the APP element are equivalent. We use uppercase as a convention for separating HTML terms from content in this book to help make the distinction clearer.

CLASS

The required CLASS attribute of the APP element defines the name of the applet to invoke at the current location in an HTML document. For example, in the previous chapter we compiled a new class called DocFooter. This is implemented in the Java file named /html/classes/DocFooter.class. Remember that the value of the CLASS attribute must be a Java class object defined in the /html/classes directory minus the .class extension, unless the SRC variable is used to specify an alternate location. For example, to invoke our DocFooter class in an HTML document, you specify the HTML as:

```
<APP CLASS="DocFooter">
```

Note that the exact spelling and capitalization of the CLASS name and its associated applet file, must be exactly as written. That's because the UNIX file system is case sensitive and, therefore, not as forgiving as the HTML specification!

SRC

The optional SRC attribute of the APP element defines the location in the server's file system where the HotJava client can find the bytecode object referenced by this attribute. The value of this attribute is a URL. The URL must contain the directory in which the class resides in its specification.

If this attribute is not specified, the HotJava client searches the directory where the current HTML document is located. For example, if the current HTML document is /html/DocFooterTest.html and includes an embedded APP element specified as <APP CLASS="DocFooter">, HotJava will look for a DocFooter class bytecode file named /html/classes/DocFooter.class.

You can also specify a remote server that contains applets you want to use. For instance, if you wanted to run an auto-emission simulation for a 4-stroke, 8-cylinder gasoline engine, you could reference an applet provided by a remote server but still supply your own set of attributes. Together, these will invoke the proper simulation. Here's a sample:

```
<APP
  CLASS="EmissionSimulation"
  SRC="http://www.nascar.org/sims/html/classes/"
  STROKE="4"
  CYLINDERS="8"
  FUEL="gasoline"
  DURATION="20secs"
  ITERATIONS="25"
>
```

The client knows that an applet is located remotely as specified by the SRC's URL value. Guess what the absolute name of the referenced applet is? Here it is:

```
http://www.nascar.org/sims/html/classes/EmissionSimulation.class
```

To Slash, or Not to Slash?

Note: The trailing slash is required when specifying the URL for the SRC attribute. For instance, this is an *invalid* specification for a SRC URL, because it lacks a closing slash:

```
SRC="doc:/demo/classes"
```

ALIGN

The optional ALIGN attribute of the APP element specifies how to orient an applet's AppletImageDisplay canvas in relation to the text flow that follows it. If the ALIGN attribute is not specified, the trailing text flow is aligned with the bottom of the canvas. This attribute can take one of these three values:

- bottom—trailing text flow is aligned with bottom of applet canvas (default)
- top—trailing text flow is aligned with the top of the applet canvas
- middle—trailing text flow is centered on the applet canvas

Here's an example that specifies that adjacent text flow is centered in the applet's canvas:

```
<APP CLASS="DocFooter" ALIGN="middle"> Align this phrase.
```

Making ALIGN Work Properly . . .

Note: If you want to get the best effect from the ALIGN attribute in the <APP> tag, don't modify the corresponding text (e.g., "Align this phrase.") with the HTML paragraph marker <P>. We weren't able to get ALIGN to work properly unless we omitted the <P> tag that preceded the text block containing <APP>.

We're not entirely sure, but this is probably browser-dependent behavior right now. Because <APP> is not standard HTML markup (it's a Sun Microsystems HTML extension), we won't know until this markup is adopted in other browsers and makes its way into an HTML DTD.

WIDTH, HEIGHT

The optional WIDTH and HEIGHT attributes control the dimensions of the applet's AppletDisplayItem canvas. The HotJava browser uses these measurements to lay out the canvas while the applet is loading into the current HTML document. The values for each of these attributes is given in pixels. For instance, this APP element specification defines the applet's canvas as 500 pixels wide by 400 pixels high:

```
<APP CLASS="DocFooter" WIDTH="500" HEIGHT="400">
```

Applet-Specific Attributes and Their Values

An APP element can take any number of applet-specific attributes. An applet is designed to accept these attributes and their corresponding values as command-line directives. The applet creator specifies the names, if any, of all attributes that may be included in an APP element. Some applets require no additional applet specific attributes, while others depend heavily upon these variable/value pairs to execute.

The inclusion of an attribute list in APP elements presents a couple of interesting problems. The first is: As an HTML author, how do you determine the applet-specific attributes for an applet you did not write? Second and more important, an all-inclusive HotJava DTD cannot be created because the dynamic nature of the attribute list for the APP element precludes a completely exhaustive treatment—which is mandatory for a DTD.

Validating HTML is becoming a vital part of the HTML document-creation process. An invalid HTML document is analogous to a C language program that compiles correctly but crashes when it runs. The HTML may look OK, but it doesn't follow the rules that the HTML DTD imposes. Don't fall into the trap of thinking that, just because an HTML browser displays a document, the document must be OK. Browsers are notoriously forgiving of HTML errors, and may even display documents with flagrant HTML mistakes or omissions.

To validate HotJava HTML documents, a definitive HotJava DTD must be created. Mark Gaither (a co-author of this book and the maintainer of HALSoft's HTML validation tool suite) created a public version of the HotJava DTD. It is an extension of the HTML 3.0 DTD that includes the APP element and its set of five attributes: class, src, align, width, and height.

It is currently impossible to declare a dynamic attribute list for this DTD like the one proposed for the APP element by the HotJava/Java developers. Although this could be overcome by creating an applet-specific HotJava DTD, it would lead to an infinite number of HotJava DTDs for each and every instance of a Java applet. A workable solution to this problem may be eventually negotiated in the course of refining the Java language. Right now, it remains unsolved.

For more information about the HotJava DTD, see this URL:

```
http://www.halsoft.com/html/
```

Applet Invocation by HotJava

As mentioned in Chapter 1, the HotJava browser operates differently from current WWW browsers such as NCSA Mosaic and Netscape Navigator. These browsers operate something like this:

- They take a URL specification and break it into its parts: protocol, host server, local information, and optional object.
- The host server and the local information (a path relative to the document root in the file system) is sent to the built-in protocol handler.
- The protocol handler creates an HTTP request that is transported across the Internet to a particular Web server.
- The server fetches the correct object and ships a stream of data that contains a MIME message body, including the requested object, back to the client.

- The client inspects the MIME Content-Type information to determine its data type and, if applicable, invokes a corresponding rendering application.

For example, an HTML document uses Content-Type=text/html, a .GIF file uses Content-Type=image/gif, and a binary object uses Content-Type=application/octet-stream.

HotJava behaves very differently. Here's what it does:

- HotJava takes as input a URL and does roughly the same thing as Mosaic or Navigator; it breaks it into constituent pieces.

- HotJava then deciphers the protocol and dynamically links the correct protocol handler into the Java runtime system. If either Netscape or Mosaic doesn't have a protocol or a MIME-type defined, these programs' configurations must be altered (or might even require the addition of new code and recompilation, in the case of a protocol change). In HotJava, a runtime connection is established as a consequence of the URL decoding process.

- While Mosaic and Netscape employ a static array of supported protocols, HotJava takes the protocol and derives a new class name. It then links in this new class. If the protocol handler class is already loaded, it uses it. If the protocol handler class is not found, HotJava looks locally for an appropriate handler. If it still can't be found, it then looks remotely at the system hosting the requested URL for the appropriate protocol handler. This is much more dynamic and open-ended than either Mosaic or Netscape.

- Finally, HotJava invokes the four private methods of the Applet class used to control the execution of a Java applet—init( ), start( ), stop( ), and destroy( ). These manage the set up and tear down of the applet during the execution process, which also includes whatever intrinsic functionality the applet itself delivers. (We have seen the mentioned methods before, in Chapter 3. As you recall, you can't explicitly call these methods; HotJava does that for you.)

Managing Applet Execution

How do HotJava and the Java runtime environment manage your applet in memory? If we examine the invocation of an Applet through HotJava's eyes, here's what we see:

- An HTML document is requested by the input of a specific URL.

- HotJava does its URL deciphering and protocol handler linking operation.

- HotJava then fetches the HTML document and scans the HTML document for an APP element.

- If it finds an APP element, HotJava fetches the applet bytecode.

- HotJava then hands the applet to the Java runtime interpreter.

- The Java interpreter checks the security of the bytecode; once the bytecode is deemed clean, the runtime system loads the class into memory.

- HotJava invokes the init( ) method if it is specified in the class. This method initializes variables, resizes its canvas, or retrieves other required resources.

- HotJava begins rendering the HTML document into its display window. After this is complete, HotJava invokes the start( ) method for the Applet if one is defined. (Remember, some applets require an external stimulus to begin execution, such as a **mouseDown** action.)

- HotJava then sits back and relaxes. When the user navigates away from the current HTML document, HotJava calls the stop( ) method if it was defined. This method will kill any active execution threads.

- After stop( ) terminates, HotJava signals the runtime system that the applet is stopped by invoking the destroy( ) method.

- The runtime system then removes the applet from memory, which halts its execution and reclaims its memory space.

This complex series of hand-offs explains how additional client-side functionality can be delivered through Java in the context of a normal HTML document. The process basically engineers the takeover of the client system while the applet runs, then returns control (and related system resources) to the invoking browser program—in this example, HotJava.

Loading Classes in the Java Runtime Environment

By default, the runtime system loads classes stored locally in files that are defined in the CLASSPATH environment variable. This activity is performed by a ClassLoader, an abstract Java class used to specify rules for loading classes into the runtime system.

Remotely-stored classes are loaded across the network and stored in an instance of the base class CLASS in the local runtime environment. This new class information is communicated to the runtime system by using the defineClass( ) method of the CLASS class. This lets local and remote classes operate (and communicate) seamlessly, and extends the capabilities of any runtime system to include whatever classes it can access, anywhere on the network.

Reloading Local Applets

When you build applets in your local file system, there's something essential to note about Alpha2 distributions: When you modify an applet, recompile it, flush HotJava's cache, and reload the HTML document, HotJava will not recognize the applet's changes. Why not? If your applet class is referenced in the CLASSPATH environment variable in the Alpha2 environment, the runtime system doesn't reload the class. In Alpha3, however, this has been fixed. But to be on the safe side, you should still follow our advice.

How, then, should you test your applets? Simply assign the CLASSPATH variable a new value and make sure you reference this change in your shell. You want to remove the path to the applet you're testing from the value of CLASSPATH. This causes HotJava to create a new instance of the class CLASS and the runtime system to load the right class. Remember, the Java runtime system uses CLASSPATH, while HotJava does not.

Two Quick HTML Examples

To familiarize you with embedding Java applets in HTML documents, we present a couple of examples. The first loads a remote Java applet while the second loads a local applet in your HTML document.

Remote Applet

This example shows how to specify an applet in an HTML document that is stored on a WWW server elsewhere on the Internet. To do this, you need to know two things.

1. You need to know the URL for the Java applet. This location on the remote server contains the Java bytecode associated with the CLASS attribute specified in the APP element.

2. You also need to know the set of attributes, including optional as well as required attributes specific to the applet.

These should be published by the applet author somewhere on the server where the remote class is stored. One programmatic solution would be for the remote class to offer a public package called Help that returns a usage statement for a specific class. This would inform the potential user of the optional and required attributes of the applet. You would make an initial query of the remote class such as:

```
<!DOCTYPE HTML PUBLIC "-//Sun Microsystems Corp.//DTD HotJava HTML//EN">
<HEAD><TITLE>Remote Applet Demo</TITLE></HEAD>
<BODY>
<H1>Remote Java Applet Demonstration</H1>
<APP CLASS="Help.RemoteClass" SRC="http://www.foo.com/classes/">
</BODY>
</HTML>
```

This could return a usage statement like the following:

```
Package: Help
    Class: RemoteClass

Attributes:
    METHOD = (one|two|three)
    SPLINE = (true|false)
    CRANK = string_value
    SPACE = integer_value
```

Now, the user has the required information to call the remote class correctly to satisfy the immediate needs of the applet and its enclosing HTML document.

Local Applet

In the next example, the compiled Java bytecode class is retrieved from your local system. To specify the correct class in the APP element of your HTML document, you need to know where the compiled class resides on your local system.

By default, if you don't specify a SRC attribute, HotJava looks for the compiled bytecode applet in a classes subdirectory beneath the current HTML document it has loaded. For example, if the current HTML document loaded into HotJava's display window is physically stored at /html/TestApplet.html and is specified as in the following code, HotJava expects to find the compiled Java applet stored at /html/classes/TestApplet.class. Your Java source code should also be specified as /html/classes/TestApplet.java.

```
<!DOCTYPE HTML PUBLIC "-//Sun Microsystems Corp.//DTD HotJava HTML//EN">
<HEAD><TITLE>Local Applet Demo</TITLE></HEAD>
<BODY>
<H1>Local Java Applet Demonstration</H1>
<APP CLASS="TestApplet">
</BODY>
</HTML>
```

You can specify the SRC attribute of the APP element to direct HotJava to look elsewhere on your local system for the compiled Java class.

The value of the SRC attribute is typically a URL. Currently, HotJava doesn't directly support specific network protocols. This is uncharacteristic of present-day WWW browsers, which are tightly bound to current network protocols such as HTTP, FTP, and GOPHER.

What HotJava does instead is link an appropriate protocol handler on demand. For example, HotJava uses the protocol specification implied in the URL to determine which protocol to link into the Java runtime system. This allows new and leading-edge protocols to be dynamically integrated into HotJava. If the correct protocol handler is not installed, the HotJava browser immediately returns to the server to retrieve the correct protocol handler for the requested object.

Here's a specification of the **doc** protocol in an APP element to retrieve a local applet:

```
<!DOCTYPE HTML PUBLIC "-//Sun Microsystems Corp.//DTD HotJava HTML//EN">
<HEAD><TITLE>Local Applet Demo</TITLE></HEAD>
<BODY>
<H1>Local Java Applet Demonstration</H1>
<APP CLASS="TestApplet" SRC="doc:/applets/">
</BODY>
</HTML>
```

The **doc** protocol is an internal protocol included with the Alpha2 and Alpha3 releases of HotJava. It is used to retrieve documents from the distribution volumes. If a document isn't found, the HotJava browser turns to http://java.sun.com/ to retrieve the document. This is similar to the Netscape **usage**: protocol is built into the Netscape Navigator browser.

Step-by-Step Installation, Testing & Use

In this section we follow each step in creating an HTML document with an embedded applet, and revive the DocFooter class example from Chapter 3.

To jog your memory, the DocFooter class appends a document footer containing information including a company logo, the date of the last revision, who made that revision, and the URL for the HTML document. Note: To ensure that the document footer is actually appended to the HTML document, you must insert the APP element in your HTML document just before the </BODY> tag that closes the document's body. In other words, you must embed the applet as the last document body element.

Actually, you could embed the DocFooter APP element anywhere in your HTML document, but then HotJava would render it according to its placement in the document flow. For example, you could make it the first element of the HTML document, but then HotJava would render it at the top of the display window. By placing it just before the </BODY> tag, you're guaranteed that it appears where it's wanted.

Step 1: Create a File Called Test.html

Change to the directory where you store your HTML documents. For this example, we call it /html. Therefore, change directories to /html and create an HTML document named Test.html with your favorite text editor.

Step 2: Insert an SGML Prolog

Now, insert an SGML prolog. This declaration contains a public identifier that specifies the HTML DTD to which the document complies, along with information about who created the DTD and the language used for the tag set.

Here is the SGML prolog for HotJava (as defined by the authors; not sanctioned by Sun Microsystems Corp.):

```
<!DOCTYPE HTML PUBLIC "-//Sun Microsystems Corp.//DTD HotJava HTML//EN">
```

This asserts that this HTML document conforms to the public HTML DTD created by Sun Microsystems Corp., which has its tag set implemented in English. This prolog is required if you intend to use other SGML tools or validation services.

Step 3: Insert the Head Matter

Next, insert the document head information. A head is the front matter of an HTML document, and often provides important identification and linkage information. Typically, the head of a document contains at least a title. For this example, specify the document head as:

```
<!DOCTYPE HTML PUBLIC "-//Sun Microsystems Corp.//DTD HotJava HTML//EN">
<HTML>
<HEAD><TITLE>My First Applet HTML Document</TITLE></HEAD>
</HTML>
```

This asserts that this document has head matter that includes a descriptive declaration of the HTML document's title.

Step 4: Insert the Document Body

Enter the body of your HTML document. This defines the content of your document. In this example, use this content markup:

```
<!DOCTYPE HTML PUBLIC "-//Sun Microsystems Corp.//DTD HotJava HTML//EN">
<HTML>
<BODY>
<H1>My First Applet HTML Document</H1>
<HR>
<P>To learn about Java, I need to create a sample HTML document.
<HR>
</BODY>
</HTML>
```

Step 5: Embed the DocFooter Applet

Add the invocation of the DocFooter applet. To do this, position your editor's insertion point immediately prior to the </BODY> tag. Add the APP element to your test HTML document. In this example, specify it as:

```
<!DOCTYPE HTML PUBLIC "-//Sun Microsystems Corp.//DTD HotJava HTML//EN">
<HTML>
<BODY>
<H1>My First Applet HTML Document</H1>
<HR>
<P>To learn about Java, I need to create a sample HTML document.
```

```
<HR>
<APP
    CLASS="DocFooter"
    LAST_UPDATED="21 Aug 95"
    EMAIL="markg@webtechs.com"
    COPY_RIGHT_NOTICE="Copyright 1995 - WebTechs. ">
</BODY>
</HTML>
```

The APP element asserts that the applet is a compiled bytecode class named DocFooter located in the classes subdirectory of the loaded HTML document. The APP element also asserts that the applet requires three applet-specific attributes, LAST_UPDATED, EMAIL, and COPY_RIGHT_NOTICE.

Step 6: Save and Load Your New HTML Document

After you save your new HTML document as a file named Test.html, load it into the HotJava browser, which is located in the distribution bin directory. After it starts, position your pointing device into the Document URL: text input box located near the top of the HotJava browser.

Select the current text in the dialog box either by depressing the left mouse button and dragging on the text or by double-clicking the text with the left mouse button. After the text is selected, enter the following file URL. (You may need to alter this URL depending where you physically store your HTML documents, Java applets, and Java classes.)

```
file:/html/Test.html
```

The HotJava browser fetches your new HTML document containing the embedded applet. If it fails to load, make sure that you've set your environment variables correctly, or explicitly specify the complete path to your HTML document.

Before your HTML document is loaded, HotJava loads the applet into memory so it can be executed by the Java runtime system. HotJava calls the init( ) method for the browser.Applet class. After HotJava loads the applet, it loads the HTML document and renders it. It then starts the applet by calling the start( ) method for the browser.Applet class.

Remember, an applet won't necessarily start executing until it receives an event. For example, an applet may require a mouseDown event from the user of the HotJava browser to begin operation. In our example, however, no outside stimulus is required. HotJava creates a canvas for our data. Finally, once the user navigates away from this document, HotJava calls the stop() and destroy() methods to terminate execution and remove the applet from memory.

Using HotJava with the Alpha2 Release

Here are a couple of tips about using both the Solaris and NT distributions of the Alpha2 release. They have been fixed in the Alpha3 release:

1. Do not run HotJava from the classes directory. Doing so doesn't function properly.

2. Reloading an HTML document after modifying and compiling a Java applet will not reload the new bytecode into memory. You have to restart the browser.

To learn about other known bugs and requested features for HotJava, see this URL:

```
http://java.sun.com/bugsandfeatures.html
```

Summary

A Java applet is embedded in an HTML document through the APP element. This element has five core attributes, but it can also support a list of applet-specific attributes. The HotJava browser implicitly calls four private methods of the Applet class to handle applet execution: init(), start(), stop(), and destroy(). The Java runtime system loads classes defined in the CLASSPATH environment variable. Together, these activities let applets do their thing within HTML documents.

In the next chapter, we dig further into the whys and wherefores of Java applets. You also will learn how to extend the functionality of existing applets and create more complex ones.

## CHAPTER 5

Extending **Applets**

he Java programming language is a new thoroughbred in the OO programming stable. Because one of OO programming's main characteristics is extensibility, this means that new functionality and features can be added to a Java class with relative ease, and such new additions are unobtrusive. They won't adversely affect other parts of an application, and the scope of such changes are localized.

Extensibility has also been shown to lower maintenance costs, while bringing new capabilities to market faster. With these weapons in its arsenal, we're expecting great things from Java. In this chapter, you'll see just how easy extending an applet can be and investigate the decision making required to decide whether extending the old, or creating anew, is the right approach to increasing your Java holdings.

Applet Analysis and Extension

A true beauty of an OO programming language is how fast you can adapt an existing class to meet new requirements. Java is no exception. You can create a new class as an extension of an existing class, add a new method, and—presto!—you have a new class with new functionality without reinventing the wheel.

New classes in Java can be extensions of any single existing class. This is called single-class inheritance, as distinguished from the multiple inheritance found in C++. (Multiple inheritance means creating a new class from more than one existing class, and is typical in many C++ implementations.) On the other hand, Java provides implementable interfaces that allow the same advantages that multiple inheritance confers, but without its nasty overhead on the system and on your overtaxed programming faculties.

With Java, the primary questions become: "When do I extend an existing applet?" versus "When do I write a new one?" The answer to these questions usually emerges following an analysis of your existing library of classes.

In such an analysis, there are three primary areas of focus that can help you to derive the correct answer to the extend-or-create dilemma. These analytical foci help you to determine the overlap or similarity among your existing classes and methods, and your new needs:

- functionality
- data handling
- interfaces and user interaction

Analyzing each of these areas helps to determine the degree of overlap between existing and planned capabilities, as well as assessing their differences. Bear in mind that some classes may possess a close match to the required functions, data handling, or interface interaction, but may also possess extra, unneeded facets. The greater these differences, the more likely it is that a new piece of code is needed.

These three foci can help you to decide if your class library possesses reusable aspects of function, data handling, and user interaction suitable for your new applet. You have to dig through each existing class to look for good candidates for a parent or superclass for your new class. Then, you must determine the similarities as well as the differences. If the differences outweigh the similarities, look further.

You may not find a class with more similarities than differences; if this happens, think hard about creating a new class from scratch. You'll extend the basic Java Object class, so you will not have to create your new class completely from scratch. But this is as close to scratch as Java gets.

This analytical process makes a strong argument for the definition of a robust and complete class library, and requires thorough design and attention to that library throughout its entire life cycle. Note also that additional intellectual effort must be expended when creating public classes, methods, interfaces, and exceptions, because of their broad availability (and, generally, their equally broad use).

If your design is properly implemented, the result should be a highly extensible class library. This permits more efficient and responsive programming efforts because it makes the components of such a library broadly applicable, much like the tools in a toolbox can be used to adjust an air conditioner and to tune up an internal combustion engine.

Extension versus Rewrite

After extensive class analysis, another alternative is to rewrite or modify an existing class to satisfy new requirements. This can be dangerous because you run the risk of affecting existing applications that already rely on this class. You need to recompile all affected applications, so this adds to your maintenance burden. In other words, proceed down this path with extreme caution!

Extension can be defined as a method of specializing an existing class to create a new class. Such a new class inherits all the public and protected methods and variables of the more general superclass.

You can think of extension of a class as specialization of that class, because you intend to change or add functionality. So, as you move down the class hierarchy, you specialize classes. As you move up the class hierarchy, you generalize classes.

The purpose of extension is to leverage the work and effort put into the existing class you intend to specialize, perhaps to solve a variation on a common problem or to play upon a common theme. The rule of thumb here is to shoot for more overlap rather than less, whether it is in the area of functionality, data handling, or interface interaction.

Rewrite is defined as substantially modifying classes, methods, constructors, or variables from an existing class. Rather than leveraging prior work, a rewrite is an extensive modification of existing code to alter its original intended use. The rule of thumb here is to require more variation than similarity, whether for functionality, data handling, or interface interaction—or all three simultaneously.

It's also a good idea to evaluate your investment in existing classes, methods, and constructors before making sweeping changes to them: If your future plans outweigh the current implementations, it's probably OK to continue down this path. If they don't, you'll probably want to take a different approach, such as defining a new set of classes, methods, and so forth, and leaving the existing ones intact.

Importing External Packages Augments Java Extensibility

Java's import feature allows you to utilize and leverage common core functionality found in the system class library. The current Java class library contains collections of classes ranging in functionality from Java language specifics to networked socket applications.

As a programmer, you can import classes like the user interface widgets to create a Java application that builds upon the common capabilities of the **Window** class found in the **awt** (abstract window toolkit) package. The same is true for the other classes in that package, and in other packages.

Even if you start from scratch when building an application, you have a wide spectrum of system library classes to build upon at your fingertips. You can quickly develop applets and applications using extensions of existing system packages and their associated classes, variables, methods, and exceptions.

For example, if you want to create your own version of an FTP client like the freeware application named *ncftp*, you could start with the core capabilities found in the system class **ftp**, which is a member of the **net** package. The effort required to create your own FTP client would then be minimal because most of the hard work would already be done.

There is, however, one noteworthy gotcha associated with importing system packages and classes. At run time, all required packages and classes for an application are loaded into the Java runtime system. If you import more classes than required, like when you specify all classes of the **awt** package (i.e., **import awt.*;**), the runtime system loads all classes in that package, resulting in a fat bytecode representation.

It's good OO programming practice to cull unnecessary imported classes. This reduces the size of your compiled class, resulting in faster execution and less memory. You could also encounter an insufficient memory condition when the runtime system loads a fat application, so be judicious.

If you're creating applets, remember that the code might wind up in someone else's runtime environment. Their run-time environment may not be a top-of-the-line computing environment (unlike yours). Be judicious here, too: If you don't need it, don't call it!

Two Applet Extension Examples

In this section, we present two simple examples of extending an applet. The first applet is an extension of the HelloWorld applet, which displays an image; the second is another extension of the same applet that plays an audio byte stream.

Here's the basic HelloWorld applet that we later modify to display an image and play audio:

```
import browser.Applet;
import awt.Graphics;

public
class HelloWorld extends Applet {
  void init() {
    resize(150,50);
  }

  public void paint(Graphics g) {
    g.drawString("Hello World!",25,25);
  }
}
```

Bringing Images and Sound to HelloWorld

Now let's extend our basic HelloWorld applet. In these examples, we create two new classes, ImageHelloWorld and AudioHelloWorld. Let's look at the first new class:

```
class ImageHelloWorld extends HelloWorld {

  Image image;  // image to display in applet

  void init() {
    super.init();
    image = getImage("images/world.gif");
  }

  public void paint(Graphics g) {
    g.drawImage(image,0,0);
  }
}
```

The class declaration asserts that this new class named ImageHelloWorld is a subclass of the class named HelloWorld. This means that the new class is a specialization of the more general class. This new class can use the protected and public variables and methods of the superclass HelloWorld.

The first method—init( )—is a protected method that the HotJava applet calls after it has loaded the applet into memory for execution. In this method, we retrieve the image data from a directory named images relative to the applet's URL. We also call the init() method of the super-class HelloWorld. This method invocation is coded as:

```
super.init();
```

The last method of this new class is called paint(Graphics), which draws the image into the applet's canvas. Pretty easy, huh?

Now let's look at our other extension to the HelloWorld applet. This class is named AudioHelloWorld; it renders an audio object in the applet's canvas rather than an image. Let's look at its specification:

```
class AudioHelloWorld extends HelloWorld {

  AudioData audio;

  void init() {
    super.init();
    audio = getAudioData("audio/helloworld.au");
  }

  void start() {
    play(audio);
  }
}
```

The class declaration asserts that a new class named AudioHelloWorld is an extension of the HelloWorld class. This also means that this new class is a specialization of a more general class.

The first method is init() again, which is quite similar to the init() method for the ImageHelloWorld class. However, it retrieves an audio data object from a directory named audio specified relative to the applet's URL. This method also calls the init( ) method for the super-class.

The next method, start( ), is one of the four methods that the HotJava browser calls automatically after an applet has been loaded into memory and all resources and variables have been initialized. HotJava calls this protected method to start the applet. In this case, the applet plays an audio byte stream to its completion.

Absorbing New Java Classes

How can you use these new classes? The first thing to do is to incorporate them into your existing HelloWorld.java file.

Here's the complete code:

```
import browser.Applet;
import browser.audio.*;
import awt.*;


public
class HelloWorld extends Applet {
  void init() {
    resize(150,50);
  }
}


class ImageHelloWorld extends HelloWorld {

  Image image;  // image to display in applet

  void init() {
    super.init();
    image = getImage("images/world.gif");
  }

  public void paint(Graphics g) {
    g.drawImage(image,0,0);
  }
}
```

```
class AudioHelloWorld extends HelloWorld {

  AudioData audio;

  void init() {
    super.init();
    audio = getAudioData("audio/helloworld.au");
  }

  void start() {
    play(audio);
  }
}
```

Next, compile this file with your Java compiler, *javac*. This creates three new files: HelloWorld.class; ImageHelloWorld.class; and, AudioHelloWorld.class.

The Java interpreter uses these new classes' bytecode files when the applet is loaded and executed by HotJava.

Next, add two APP elements to your HelloWorld.html document:

```
<APP CLASS="ImageHelloWorld">
<APP CLASS="AudioHelloWorld">
```

Now, you're ready to do some real testing!

Step-by-Step Extension Testing & Use

In this section, we take you through a step-by-step extension of the DocFooter class introduced in Chapter 3. For review, here's the DocFooter Java source code:

```
import browser.*; // import all items of browser system package
import awt.*; // import all items of awt system package
import net.www.html.*;

public class DocFooter extends Applet {

  // declaration of instance variables
  String date; // date of last update
  String email; // author's e-mail address
```

```
String copyright; // copyright blurb
Image logo; // .GIF image of company logo

// method invoked by HotJava to initialize the applet
protected void init() {
    resize(500,100); // 500 pixels wide & 100 pixels high canvas
    logo = getImage("images/logo.gif"); // retrieve .GIF file

    // get applet attributes from <APP> tag
    date = getAttribute("LAST_UPDATED");
    email = getAttribute("EMAIL");
    copyright = getAttribute("COPY_RIGHT_NOTICE");
}

// definition of the paint() method of the DocFooter class
public void paint(Graphics g) {

    // render the logo image in the canvas
    // originate image at upper left corner of canvas
    g.drawImage(logo,0,0);

    // render string data into the canvas at specific spots
    g.drawString(date + " by ",100,15);
    g.drawString(email,290,15);
    g.drawString(copyright,100,35);

    // get the URL of the document with the embedded <APP> tag
    URL url = new URL(documentURL,"");

    // convert the url to a string of typical representation
    String urlstring = url.toExternalForm();

    // render the URL string to the canvas
    g.drawString(urlstring,100,55);
    }
}
```

The purpose of this exercise is to create a new and specialized class named DynamicDocFooter. This new class does the same thing as the

DocFooter class, but the new class also retrieves copyright information from a data file.

Step 1: Open DocFooter.java File

With your favorite text editor, open the DocFooter.java source code file we created previously. This example assumes that this file is found in the /html/classes directory, which is also where the compiled class objects exist. Therefore, the absolute path for the Java source code file you will edit is /html/classes/DocFooter.java.

Step 2: Add New Class Declaration

In this step, you add a new class to your DocFooter Java source code file. Enter the following class declaration:

```
class DynamicDocFooter extends DocFooter {


}
```

This asserts that you're declaring a new class named DynamicDocFooter as an extension to the existing class named DocFooter (a specialization of a more general class). The new class inherits all public and protected variables and methods from its parent or superclass (i.e., DocFooter).

Step 3: Declare Instance Variables

In this step, you declare instance variables necessary for the new class. The only variable we need describes the random access data file that contains the copyright notice text. This example assumes that this is a single line in a file named /tmp/copyrght.txt that reads: "Copyright 1995. All rights reserved." Thus, add this declaration of the instance variable to the new class declaration:

```
public RandomAccessFile file;
```

Step 4: Add the init() Method

In this step, you add the init() method that HotJava calls implicitly on your behalf. In this method, we call the init() method of the superclass. In addition, we define a new variable to represent the RandomAccessFile object. Thus, you enter this code into the body of the new class declaration:

```
protected void init() {
  super.init();
  file = new RandomAccessFile(copyright,"r");
}
```

The file variable is of type RandomAccessFile. Its constructor takes two strings: the copyright string takes the value of the COPY_RIGHT_NOTICE attribute of the APP element for the DocFooter class, and the "r" means the file is read only.

Step 5: Add the paint() Method

In this step, you add the paint() method for the new class. It is quite similar to the paint() method of the superclass except that you retrieve the copyright notice text from a file in the file system instead of supplying it as an input string. The location of this file is the value supplied for the APP attribute COPY_RIGHT_NOTICE in the calling HTML document. Here's the code:

```
public void paint(Graphics g) {

  g.drawImage(logo,0,0);
  g.drawString(date + " by ",100,15);
  g.drawString(email,290,15);

  // read a line from the file as a string
  String copyright = file.readLine();

  URL url = new URL(documentURL,"");
  String urlstring = url.toExternalForm();
  g.drawString(urlstring,100,55);
}
```

Step 6: Save New DocFooter.java File

In this step, you save the new class declaration in the DocFooter.java file. Here's the complete Java source code file with the new class declaration and implementation:

```
import browser.*; // import all items of browser system package
import awt.*; // import all items of awt system package
import net.www.html.*;
```

```
import java.io.*;
public class DocFooter extends Applet {

  // declaration of instance variables
  String date; // date of last update
  String email; // author's e-mail address
  String copyright; // copyright blurb
  Image logo; // .GIF image of company logo

  // method invoked by HotJava to initialize the applet
  protected void init() {
    resize(500,100); // 500 pixels wide & 100 pixels high canvas
    logo = getImage("images/logo.gif"); // retrieve .GIF file

    // get applet attributes from <APP> tag
    date = getAttribute("LAST_UPDATED");
    email = getAttribute("EMAIL");
    copyright = getAttribute("COPY_RIGHT_NOTICE");
  }
  // definition of the paint() method of the DocFooter class
  public void paint(Graphics g) {

    // render the logo image in the canvas
    // originate image at upper left corner of canvas
    g.drawImage(logo,0,0);

    // render string data into the canvas at specific spots
    g.drawString(date + " by ",100,15);
    g.drawString(email,290,15);
    g.drawString(copyright,100,35);

    // get the URL of the document with the embedded <APP> tag
    URL url = new URL(documentURL,"");

    // convert the url to a string of typical representation
    String urlstring = url.toExternalForm();
```

```
    // render the URL string to the canvas
    g.drawString(urlstring,100,55);
  }


  // declare a new public subclass of DocFooter
  class DynamicDocFooter extends DocFooter {

    public RandomAccessFile file;

    protected void init() {
        super.init();
        file = new RandomAccessFile(copyright,"r");
    }

    public void paint(Graphics g) {

        g.drawImage(logo,0,0);
        g.drawString(date + " by ",100,15);
        g.drawString(email,290,15);

        // read a line from the file as a string
        String copyright = file.readLine();
        g.drawString( cpyright, 150, 55);

        URL url = new URL(documentURL,"");
        String urlstring = url.toExternalForm();
        g.drawString(urlstring,100,55);
    }
  }
}
```

Step 7: Compile the New Class

In this step, you compile the new class into a Java class that takes the
filename /html/classes/DocFooter.class. On the command line, type:

```
javac DocFooter.java
```

If this is successful, you will find two Java bytecode files in the
/html/classes/ directory named DocFooter.class and
DynamicDocFooter.class. Otherwise, check your code and recompile.

Step 8: Edit DocFooter.html File

In this step, you add the proper class attribute to the APP element in the DocFooter.html document. For this example, the file is found in the /html directory, so the full path for this HTML document is /html/DocFooter.html.

Using your text editor, add this APP element to the DocFooter.html document:

```
<APP
  CLASS="DynamicDocFooter"
  LAST_UPDATED="21 Aug 95"
  EMAIL="markg@webtechs.com"
  COPY_RIGHT_NOTICE="/tmp/cpyrght.txt"
>
```

Here's the complete HTML document entitled DocFooter.html:

```
<!DOCTYPE HTML PUBLIC "-//Sun Microsystems Corp.//DTD HTML//EN">
<HTML>
<HEAD><TITLE>Test Applet</TITLE></HEAD>
<BODY>
<H1>My First Applet HTML Document</H1>
<HR>
<P> To learn about Java, I need to create a sample HTML document.
<HR>
<APP
  CLASS="DynamicDocFooter"
  LAST_UPDATED="21 Aug 95"
  EMAIL="markg@webtechs.com"
  COPY_RIGHT_NOTICE="/tmp/cpyrght.txt"
>
</BODY>
</HTML>
```

Step 9: Load DocFooter.html into HotJava

In this step, you load the new HTML document into HotJava. Start HotJava, then in the Document URL: input text widget enter the URL for the DocFooter.html document. In this example, this is:

```
file:/html/DocFooter.html
```

Hit the Return key, and the HotJava browser retrieves the URL, loads the DynamicDocFooter class into the Java runtime system, initializes any required resources and variables of the applet, renders the HTML document, and starts any required threads. Finally, HotJava renders the applet onto its canvas.

Figure 5–1 shows what you should see:

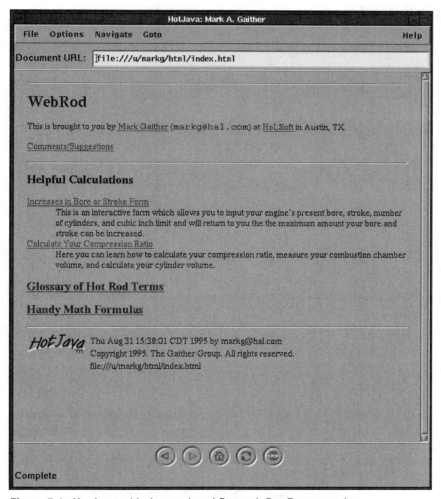

Figure 5-1: HotJava with the rendered DynamicDocFooter applet

Summary

Java applets can be specialized to include new functionality, new data and data handling methods, or new user interface interactions from more general classes. This is known as extending a class. Extending a class allows you to quickly adapt common core capabilities in existing classes. It can greatly speed development time, especially when the functionality you need can be used from predefined system classes or packages, or from existing code.

In the next chapter, we introduce you to a full-blown Java application. Unlike a Java applet that you invoke from within another program or an HTML document, these applications function as completely stand-alone software systems.

Section Three

Advanced Java Applications

*t*he third tutorial here in Section 3 includes discussions of compiling and running Java applications and of how to extend existing Java applications, and an examination of a Java Protocol handler. Section 3 concludes with a speculative rumination on Java's present and future capabilities.

Chapter 6 covers the ins and outs of designing and building a Java application. Chapter 7, Compiling and Running an Application, explores the capabilities and the use of the Java runtime environment. Chapter 8, Extending Java Applications, analyzes the efforts involved in extending existing Java objects, classes, methods, and constructors. Your in-depth exposure to the Java language concludes with Chapter 9, A Java Protocol Handler, which provides a detailed exposition of the requirements, design, and implementation of a new, dynamic networking protocol for the Web, including its associated document and data types.

After a look at these Java implementations, we turn speculative in Chapter 10, The Future of Java. Here, we explore Java's potential and try to recommend appropriate applications based on its current capabilities. After a broad discussion of Java's current drawbacks and shortcomings, we cover ongoing research and implementation directions for both Java and related development environments and tools. Throughout, we refer to concrete examples and point to accessible Web sites wherever possible. Finally, we supply a compendium of useful Java-related Web resources to help readers who are interested in learning more to find the latest and greatest information about Java in particular and WWW programming in general.

## CHAPTER 6

Writing and Using Java Applications

*i*n this chapter, you learn how to write a stand-alone Java application. A stand-alone application is different from the applet we presented in Section 2. An applet's execution is controlled by the HotJava browser: The browser initiates execution from the Java runtime system after the HTML document passes the URL included in the <APP> tag back to the Web server. On the other hand, a stand-alone Java application requires no external mediation. It controls its own execution and communicates directly with the Java runtime system.

The HotJava browser is the archetypal example of a Java application. Written in Java, it interacts with the Java runtime system to execute. Applications like the HotJava browser are run from the command line rather than being launched from within HotJava, as in the case of an applet.

In this chapter, we begin by describing the concept for a Java application. Next, we perform a crude requirements analysis and create an overall design. Finally, we step through the code that results from these efforts. Keep in mind that this is a representative example; not all your Java applications will be this easy to build!

Application Concept

In this section, we present an overall concept for a simple but powerful stand-alone Java application. This application offers only limited functionality, but it could provide a basis for you to extend.

The Java application you'll create is called RenderImageApp. When executed from the command line, RenderImageApp brings up a window entitled "Render a Local Image." Within this main window, you'll include two other types of window elements. The first is a text input widget that allows users to enter a local URL for an image. The second is a drawing canvas where the image can be rendered by the application.

The application ensures that the local image URL specified is valid. If it's not, a message is printed to the standard error file handle, known as STDERR in UNIX environments. By default, the first image rendered will be the HotJava logo .GIF image.

Writing a Java Application, Step by Step

In this section, we guide you through each step in creating RenderImageApp. Within each step, you find a detailed explanation for each line of code, so you will be clear about its meaning and purpose.

Step 1: Create a File Named RenderImageApp.java and Import Required System Packages

In this step, create a file named RenderImageApp.java in the /html/classes directory. Therefore, the full path for your new application is /html/classes/RenderImageApp.java.

Next, specify the system packages and classes your application will incorporate, using the **import** keyword. Here's the code:

```
// Import all required system packages
import awt.*;              // Abstract Window Toolkit package
import java.lang.*;        // Java language package
import browser.*;          // HotJava package
import net.www.html.*;     // HTML document package
import java.io.*;          // Java input/output package
```

Step 2: Declare New Class RenderImageApp

In this section, you declare a new class named **RenderImageApp**. This new class is an extension to the system class named **Frame**. Let's look at the declaration:

```
public class RenderImageApp extends Frame {
    ... body of class ..
}
```

From this declaration, you see that your new class is an extension to the existing **Frame** class, making **Frame** its superclass. With this extension, you inherit all of **Frame**'s public and protected class variables, its constructors, and its methods.

Step 3: Declare Instance and Class Variables

In this section, you declare your class and instance variables. A class variable is always declared **static** and is visible to other classes, while instance variables pertain only to a particular instance of a given class. Here are the declarations:

```
// Class variables
static WServer server = null; // window server
static Frame frame;           // main container frame
static Font labelFont;        // font of label on text widget
static inputWindow iw;        // input window object
static renderWindow rw;       // canvas where image is rendered


// Instance variables
URL imgURL;                   // URL of image to render
```

Step 4: Create the Constructor

In this section, you declare the constructor for the new **RenderImageApp** class. This is a public constructor, which means that other classes in the system can create new objects of this type (i.e., **RenderImageApp**). The purposes of this public constructor are:

- to set the text for the title on the display frame;
- to set the desired font size and font family for any labels on the display frame; and

121

- to map the input and render window elements into the main frame.

Here's the code:

```
/* Public constructor, which takes two arguments. The first is the
current window server and the second is an array of any command line
arguments specified by the user when starting the application. */
public RenderImageApp(WServer serv, String args[]) {

  /* This calls the constructor of superclass Frame. This line
  creates a Frame object, associates it with the current window
  server (serv), and gives the object a title bar (true). This
  frame has no parent frame (null), the frame is 400 pixels wide and
  500 pixels high, and the background color of the frame is light
  gray. */
  super(serv,true,null,400,500,Color.lightGray);

  /* This sets the title of the main display frame to the specified
  string value. Notice that it calls the public method of the
  superclass Frame. */
  super.setTitle("Render an Image");

  /* This gets a plain Helvetica font of size 12 from the current
  window server. This line assigns a Font type to a class
  variable named labelFont by calling the public method
  serv.fonts.getFont(String,int,int). This method's qualifiers are
  the current window server serv, the class variable fonts, which
  is a FontTable type of object, and getFont, which is a public
  method of the FontTable class. */
  labelFont = serv.fonts.getFont("Helvetica",Font.PLAIN,12);

  /* This section of code initializes the class varible imgURL.
  This is the URL of the first image rendered. You can specify an
  alternate initial image on the command line when starting this
  application. If the array args[] has a length greater than zero,
  the string specified as args[0] is used as the initial image. */
  if(args.length > 0) {
    imgURL = new URL(null,args[0]);
  }
```

```
else {
   imgURL = new URL(null,"file:/html/images/logo.gif");
}


/* This line creates an input text widget window where users enter
a URL*/
iw = new inputWindow(this,this.labelFont);


/* This line realizes the display canvas where an image is
rendered into the main display frame */
rw = new renderWindow(this,imgURL);


/* This is a public method of the Frame class which maps new
elements into the main display frame. */
map();
}
```

We should clarify further how the constructor gets the 12-point
Helvetica font from the window server. The current window server is
passed to the constructor through the parameter list as serv of type
WServer. The **WServer** class has a public class variable named **fonts**,
a variable of type **FontTable** class from the **awt** package.

The **FontTable** class contains a public method named
getFont(String,int,int) that returns a platform-specific font specified
by a generic font family name (e.g., Times or Helvetica). Table 6-1 summarizes what's involved in obtaining a generic font.

Table 6-1: Generic Font Specification

OBJECT	TYPE	DESCRIPTION
serv	WServer	current window server
serv.fonts	FontTable	class variable from WServer class
serv.fonts.getFont	Font	public method from the FontTable class; returns a Font

Step 5: Create the main Method

In this step, you create the main method for the new **RenderImageApp** class. This particular method differentiates an applet from an application. The main method controls execution of the Java application and is therefore also absent from an applet. The main method is always declared as **public** and **static**. Here's the code:

```
// main procedure of RenderImageApp class
public static void main(String args[]) {
   ... body of main procedure ...
}
```

In this example, the return type for the main method is **null**. This method is like a procedure rather than a function, which usually returns a value. Its one parameter is an array of strings, each of which is a command-line option that's specified when the **RenderImageApp** application is invoked.

In this example, you can specify the initial image to be rendered by **RenderImageApp** on the command line, such as:

```
java RenderImageApp file:/html/images/warning.gif
```

The file:/html/images/warning.gif is an optional command-line option. If it's not supplied, the HotJava logo image is rendered on the application's canvas. In the preceding invocation of **RenderImageApp**, the length of the **args[]** array is one, and its only cell takes the following value:

```
args[0] = "file:/html/images/warning.gif"
```

As in C and C++, an array index begins with 0. Our application checks the value of **args[0]**. If it is null, the default image is rendered; otherwise, the image specified on the command line is rendered.

Step 6: Specify main Implementation

In this step, you complete the implementation of the main method. In this example, we create and start a new window server. Finally, we create an instance of the **RenderImageApp** class, which becomes an executable Java application.

Here's the implementation for **main**:

```
public static void main(String args[]) {
```

```
/* Create a window server object. This provides an API to the
native windowing system. */
server = new WServer();

/* Start the new window server by calling a public method
called start. This initializes the API to the native windowing
system. */
server.start();

/* Create an instance of the RenderImageApp class. This is our new
Java application. The RenderImageApp public constructor is called
with two arguments, the new window server object that has been
started and the command line arguments, if any. */
RenderImageApp ri = new RenderImageApp(server,args);
}
```

The main method controls the execution of our Java application, much like the main procedure in a C program. The main method calls other functions or procedures from within its execution unit. In Java, rather than calling other methods, the main method is typically used to create new instances of classes belonging to the execution unit.

Here's the declaration and specification for the **RenderImageApp** class:

```
// Import all required system packages
import awt.*;              // Abstract Window Toolkit package
import java.lang.*;        // Java language package
import browser.*;          // HotJava package
import net.www.html.*;     // HTML document package
import java.io.*;          // Java input/output package


public class RenderImageApp extends Frame {

    // Class variables
    static WServer server = null;  // window server
    static Frame frame;            // main container frame
    static Font labelFont;         // font of label on text widget
    static inputWindow iw;         // input window object
    static renderWindow rw;        // canvas where image is rendered
```

```
// Instance variables
URL imgURL;                         // URL of image to render

/* The public constructor takes two arguments. The first is the
current window server; the second is an array of command line
arguments. */
public RenderImageApp(WServer serv, String args[]) {

  /* This calls the constructor for superclass Frame. */
  super(serv,true,null,400,500,Color.lightGray);

  /* This sets the title of the main display frame to the specified
  string value. */
  super.setTitle("Render an Image");

  /* This gets a plain Helvetica font of size 12 from the current
  window server. */
  labelFont = serv.fonts.getFont("Helvetica",Font.PLAIN,12);

  /* This code initializes the class varible imgURL. */
  if(args.length > 0) {
    imgURL = new URL(null,args[0]);
  }
  else {
    imgURL = new URL(null,"file:/html/images/logo.gif");
  }

  /* This creates an input text widget window to enter a URL. */
  iw = new inputWindow(this,this.labelFont);

  /* Places the display canvas into the main display frame */
  rw = new renderWindow(this,imgURL);

  /* This public method of the Frame class maps new elements into
  the main display frame. */
  map();
}

// main method of the new class
```

```
public static void main(String args[]) {

    /* Creates a window server object; provides an API to the native
    windowing system. */
    server = new WServer();

    /* Starts the new window server */
    server.start();

    /* Creates instance of the RenderImageApp class. */
    RenderImageApp ri = new RenderImageApp(server,args);
}
}
```

Step 7: Declare a New Class Named renderWindow

In this step, you add the declaration and implementation of a new class used by the **RenderImageApp** class to the RenderImageApp.java file. With the RenderImageApp.java file loaded in your text editor, declare a new class named **renderWindow**. You can declare **renderWindow** anywhere in the file. In our example, we enter the code for this new class immediately after the declaration of the **RenderImageApp** class.

This new class, **renderWindow**, is an extension of the system class named **Window**. **Window** is a general-purpose unit that can contain other units, especially other windows. The purpose of **renderWindow** is to provide a canvas for the **RenderImageApp** application. The **renderWindow** canvas lies beneath the window that contains the input text widget. (This window object will be defined in step 8.)

The **renderWindow** class has one public constructor, and one public method that paints the image into the **renderWindow** canvas. The constructor calls the constructor for the superclass **Window**. The paint method opens a named input stream of image data and renders it into the **renderWindow** canvas area, which is 400 pixels wide by 400 pixels high, using the background color from the parent frame.

In our example, the parent frame is the **RenderImageApp** class. The paint method renders the image near the approximate center of the canvas.

127

Here's the class declaration for **renderWindow**:

```
/* Declare a new class used by RenderImageApp named renderWindow.
This window is the drawing canvas for the RenderImageApp
application. This new class is an extension of the system class
named Window. */
class renderWindow extends Window {

  // Declare instance variables. There are no class variables.
  URL u;
  // URL for image entered into the text widget
  InputStream istream;
  // named input stream of image data
  Image image;
  // image object to be rendered

  /* Declare the public constructor. It takes two arguments, the
  parent frame of the renderWindow and the URL of the image data. */
  public renderWindow(Frame frame, URL url) {

    /* Call the constructor of the superclass named Window. It takes
    five arguments: the parent frame that contains a renderWindow, the
    name of the Window, the background color of the parent frame, and
    the width and height in pixels. */
    super(frame,"Center",frame.background,400,400);

    /* Initialize the URL instance variable passed as an argument to
    the constructor */
    u = url;
  }

  /* Declare a public method named paint to render the image into
  the renderWindow canvas. This method will open a named input
  stream of image data and create an Image object from this data
  stream. */
  public void paint() {

    /* Open a named input stream. This is a public method of the
    URL class. */
    istream = u.openStream();
```

```
/* Create a new Image object. The createImage public method
belongs to the Window class. The version of the public method used
below takes one argument, which is a GifImage object. The GifImage
class is a part of the awt package and is an extension of the
DIBitmap class, which is a device independent bitmap. The
constructor for the GifImage class takes as one argument an input
stream that is both named and opened. In our example, this data
stream contains the image data. */
image = createImage(new GifImage(istream));

/* Now determine the set of x and y coordinates for the upper-left
corner of the image. The width and height of the image can be
accessed through the Image class variables of the same names. */
int x = 200 - image.width;
int y = 200 - image.height;

/* Draw the image at the calculated x and y coordinates. This is
a public method for the Window class.*/
drawImage(image,x,y);
    }
}
```

Step 8: Declare a New Class Named inputWindow

In this step, you declare and implement another new class used by the
RenderImageApp, named **inputWindow**. The **inputWindow** class
contains three elements: an input text widget, a label for this widget,
and a horizontal rule. The **inputWindow** class is an extension of the
system class named Window, just like the **renderWindow** class.

The **inputWindow** class contains three elements, two of which are
contained in a **TextField** object. These two elements, the label and the
input text widget, are laid out as row elements. This means that they
are managed and rendered as row elements—that is, they're assembled
and rendered horizontally. Finally, the label element uses blue text to
distinguish it from other items belonging to the application.

The **inputWindow** class uses one public constructor that takes two
arguments. The first is the parent frame of the **inputWindow** object.
It also takes the specified font for the **RenderImageApp** class. This
class also has one public method named paint, which renders a small,

three-dimensional horizontal rule positioned directly beneath the **TextField** object that serves as a separator between the input window and the rendering canvas.

Here's the declaration and implementation of the **inputWindow** class:

```
/* Declare a new class named inputWindow as an extension of the system
class named Window. This class contains three elements: one input text
widget with its label and a separator horizontal rule drawn as a three
dimensional image. */
class inputWindow extends Window {

  // Declare class variables
  public TextField uf; // input text widget
  public URL imgurl;   // URL of image

  // Declare instance variables
  Label urlTitle;        // label of input text widget

  /* Declare a public constructor that takes two arguments. The
  first argument is the parent frame and the second is the font of
  the RenderImageApp class. Our constructor calls the constructor of
  the superclass Window with five arguments. */
  public inputWindow(Frame frame, Font font) {

    /* Call the constructor of the superclass Window. This takes five
    arguments: the parent frame, the name of the window, the
    background color of the parent frame, and the width and height of
    the inputWindow in pixels. */
    super(frame,"North",frame.background,100,100);

    /* Manage the layout of window elements as rows of elements. The
    setLayout public method belongs to the Container class of the
    awt package. It manages the layout of elements of type
    ContainerLayout. The RowLayout constructor creates a
    ContainerLayout object. */
    setLayout(new RowLayout(true));

  /* Create a column element in the first row. This column contains a
  chunk of whitespace and the label of the input text
```

widget. The constructor takes three arguments: the current inputWindow object, no specified name, and don't center the column. */

```
Column col = new Column(this,null,false);
```

/* Now, create white space 10 pixels wide and seven pixels high. This aligns the label with the center of the input text widget to be rendered later in this method. This constructor takes six arguments: the parent container, no specified name, the width and height in pixels, no horizontal and no vertical fill. */

```
new Space(col,null,10,7,false,false);
```

/* Create a new label for the input text widget. The constructor takes as arguments: the text of the label, no name for this element, parent window of this element, and the font used for the label. */

```
urlTitle = new Label("Image:",null,col,font);
```

/* Set the color of the label text using a class variable of the Color system class as the argument passed to the public method setColor from the Label class.*/

```
urlTitle.setColor(Color.blue);
```

/* Create the input text widget. This is a new class named urlField. The constructor takes three arguments: the initial text displayed in the widget, the parent container of this element, and the parent frame element that has been cast to match the RenderImageApp class.*/

```
uf = new urlField("",this,(RenderImageApp)frame);
```

/* Turn on horizontal fill for the input text widget. This will stretch the entire row from left to right margins. */

```
uf.setHFill(true);
}
```

/* Declare a public method name paint. This method paints a small, three-dimensional horizontal rule that separates the input and render windows. */

```
public void paint() {
```

```
/* This public method of the Window class takes six arguments: x
and y coordinates for the upper-left corner of the rectangle, the
width and height of the rectangle in pixels, the rectangle is not
filled and is not raised. The variables width and height are class
variables of the Window class.*/
paint3DRect(0,height-2,width,2,false,false);
    }
}
```

Step 9: Declare the urlField Input Text Widget Class

In this step, you declare and implement a class named **urlField**. This new class is an extension of the **TextField** system class, an input text widget in which users can enter text. An instance of the **urlField** class is rendered as an element of an **inputWindow** instance.

This new class has one public constructor that takes three arguments. The first is a **String** value to contain the initialized text for the input text widget. (In our case, we don't require an initialized text string.) The second argument is the parent window of the **urlField** element. In this case, the parent window is an instance of **inputWindow**. The third argument is an instance of the **RenderImageApp** class. The urlField class also has one public method named selected. This method is called when the Enter key is depressed while an instance of **urlField** has the focus. In other words, selected is called after a user types text into the input text widget and hits Enter. This method clears the rendering canvas and then attempts to render the image specified by the new URL in the input text widget.

If the URL entered by the user in the input text widget can't be found, an exception is raised and the application prints an error message to the STDERR file handle. These messages will appear in the window in which you first launched your application. If the URL is found, it is rendered into the renderWindow canvas.

Here's the declaration and implementation of the **urlField** class. (Enter the code just after the **inputWindow** class declaration and implementation.)

```
/* Declare a new class used by RenderImageApp named urlField. This is
an extension of the system class named TextField. This input widget
accepts text input from the user. */
class urlField extends TextField {
```

```java
// Declare instance variables
RenderImageApp r;   // an instance of our Java application
URL u;              // URL of image


// Constructor
public urlField(String value, Window parent, RenderImageApp ri) {

  /* Call the constructor of the superclass TextField. It takes
  four arguments: a default text string value, name of this
  component, the parent window, and if the widget is editable. */
  super(value,null,parent,true);

  /* Set the color and font of the text of the input text widget.
  These are public methods of the TextField class in the awt
  package.*/
  setColor(Color.black);
  setFont(ri.labelFont); // font of RenderImageApp instance

  /* Realize instance variable */
  r = ri;
}


/* This is a public method that accepts text in an input text
widget, clears the current image from the canvas, and paints
the new image in the renderWindow canvas.*/
public void selected() {

  /* Clear the canvas. This calls a public method of the Window
  class. It takes four arguments: the x and y coordinates of the
  upper-left corner of the image, and the width and height of the
  image. The rw value is a static and public renderWindow class
  variable of the RenderImageApp class.*/
  r.rw.clearRect(0,0,r.rw.width,r.rw.height);

  /* Create a new URL and assign it to a renderWindow instance
  variable, u. The public method, getText(), is a member of the
  TextField class. The URL constructor takes two arguments: a URL
  context and a relative URL. In this example, the context of the
```

133

```
URL is null. */
r.rw.u = new URL(null,getText());

/* Trap for exceptions if the URL entered into the input text
widget is not found. The public method paint() is a member of the
renderWindow class. IOException is a class in the java.lang
package.*/
try {
  r.rw.paint(); // paint the image
}
catch(IOException e) {
  System.err.println("Unable to retrieve URL.");
}
  }
}
```

Step 10: Save and Compile RenderImageApp.java

In this step, you begin by saving the four new classes you just entered into your text editor. Save the file as RenderImageApp.java in the /html/classes directory.

Next, you compile your new RenderImageApp Java application. Change directories to /html/classes and invoke the Java compiler while in this directory of your new application. The command is:

```
javac RenderImageApp.java
```

Once this compiles successfully, you have the following four new classes in the /html/classes directory:

- RenderImageApp.class—our application
- renderWindow.class—the image canvas
- inputWindow.class—the window containing the URL input text widget
- urlField.class—the input text widget

Step 11: Run Your New Application

To execute your new Java application, you must run the Java interpreter against the RenderImageApp.class file in the /html/classes directory. When executing your new bytecode in the Java runtime system, discard the extension .class when specifying the application on the command line.

To run your new application with the default initial image, enter the following on the command line, after you're situated in the /html/classes directory:

```
java RenderImageApp &
```

This runs the Java interpreter, *java*, on a Java class named RenderImageApp in the background shell. To run your application with a different initial image, specify the URL for an image on the command line like this:

```
java RenderImageApp file:/html/images/monkey.gif &
```

This renders a .GIF image contained in the file monkey.gif rather than the hard-coded HotJava logo .GIF image on the image canvas.

Summary

A Java application differs from a Java applet in its use of an explicit main method that controls its overall execution. Applications are stand-alone programs that may be used for windowing applications, shell-level programs, or even CGI programs. In short, they do just about anything you want!

In the next chapter, you learn how to take advantage of Java's power and networking abilities as we investigate how to manage its development process. Soon, you'll be able to tackle Java projects completely on your own!

## CHAPTER 7

Managing Java
Applications

*a*s an OO programming language, one of Java's main characteristics is its extensibility. Reusability is another of Java's OO characteristics that's strongly related to extensibility. Inherent in good OO programming techniques, reusability dangles the tantalizing possibility for easy and regular reuse of code. Unfortunately, both of these OO buzzwords can cause major project management headaches.

One saving grace is the concept of a library of core elements. In Java, this is represented by a collection of packages. Remember, a Java package is just a named collection of similar classes that are similar in functionality, data, or interface interaction. For example, the net package in the Java system library contains classes related to distributed networking. Likewise, the java.io package contains classes that deal with Java input and output constructs. In this chapter, you learn why it's crucial to develop a robust library of classes upon which you can build. Even more important, you learn how to use such libraries effectively. You also learn more about the Java compiler in glorious detail. We even show you how to create and install an application wrapper script to provide a straightforward, simple interface to your Java applications. Finally, we guide you through the step-by-step compilation and installation of the Java application named RenderImageApp that you created in the preceding chapter.

Managing Class Libraries & Java Applications

In this section, we explain why it's so important to effectively manage and organize your Java applications. We also propose a hypothetical organization for your class library's structure.

In the Java runtime environment, the system class library is located in a particular place in the file system. This can be where the install script puts it, but it can also be where you explicitly place it. For example, the root directory for the system class library of the Alpha3 distribution is defined as follows. (<My_path> is where you put the distribution in your file system.)

```
<my_path>/hotjava/classes/
```

Beneath this directory are four subdirectories that represent the four top-level Java packages (i.e., **awt, browser, java,** and **net**) in the system class library:

```
<my_path>/hotjava/classes/awt
<my_path>/hotjava/classes/browser
<my_path>/hotjava/classes/java
<my_path>/hotjava/classes/net
```

These packages are always included as a part of your CLASSPATH environment variable, so you don't have to include them yourself. This appears to work entirely automatically, but in reality it's not automatic; it's programmatically controlled through a wrapper script that we introduce later in this chapter.

What if you wanted to develop your own library of classes for others to use? First, you should make sure that you're not duplicating classes and methods provided in the system class library. If you feel sure that you need a library of entirely new classes, you should design it carefully. The judicious design and organization of classes into packages can pay off handsomely in the long run. But poorly designed libraries can contain inconsistencies or overlaps that might introduce the Java compiler to ambiguities or conflicting definitions that it cannot correctly resolve.

The first step in creating your own library of classes is to determine where to install it in your file system. It should be in a well-known public area such as /usr/local/mylib/classes. The possibility that this path is already part of your user community's path is fairly high, so it makes a good candidate for the location of your new class library. You might also use a company-wide tools directory like /usr/tools/mylib/classes; this location is also good for your new library.

The next step is to design your new library. Let's say you're building a library of classes for a simulator. The simulator requires input, output, controls, and utilities. Consequently, the following associated packages provide a reasonable point of departure:

```
Simulator.input
Simulator.output
Simulator.controls
Simulator.utils
```

Within each of these packages, you must define classes, each with its own distinct methods and variables. Remember, though, that each class is a descendent (direct or indirect) of a single super class, **java.lang.Object**.

For a real-world example of a nice, neat collection of Java packages, look at the Web site at WebLogic Technologies, a San Francisco-based company. They've developed a tool named WebScript® that aids the integration of the Web with existing business applications and databases. They've developed three packages:

```
webscript.dblayer
webscript.html
webscript.utils
```

Each package contains classes, and their methods and variables, with each providing some specific capability. For instance, the **webscript.dblayer** package contains classes like **Database**, **DataSet**, **Column**, **Record**, and **Table**. These classes represent typical objects (or their structural equivalents) found in most relational database systems.

For a closer look at the WebLogic site, consult either of these URLs:

```
http://www.weblogic.com/
http://weblogic.com/webscript/tutorial/toc.html
```

You could do much worse than to organize the classes in your packages in a similar fashion. To begin, you need to determine the real-world and abstract objects your applications require.

For instance, in the example **Simulator** class library, you could look at the simulator as a real-world object and choose other real-world objects that either complement or comprise a simulator. This is called decomposing an object—a classical approach to OO design—that involves breaking one object into smaller constituent objects. Decomposition can facilitate development of a comprehensive library of classes.

Don't forget to include abstract objects when decomposing your classes. These are things you cannot see or put your finger on, but they still exist and can be valuable parts of your class library. For example, the **Thread** class of the system package **java.lang** is an abstract but viable part of the package. It controls the allocation of execution units from the system and helps you control how well (and how fast) your application executes.

Finally, when developing a new library of classes, you should provide a package declaration on the first noncomment line for each class in the package. Here's an example:

```
package Simulator.input;


import java.lang.*;



public class getData {
   ... body of class ...
}
```

The class **getData** is made a member of the **Simulator.input** package by the declaration in the preceding Java code fragment.

Compiling Java Applications

In this section, you learn more about compiling your Java applications. Much of this information can also be applied to Java applets.

The Java compiler, *javac*, compiles each class specified in Java code into its bytecode representation; it compiles any file with a .java extension into a binary object file with a .class extension. This new binary object can now be interpreted by the Java interpreter, *java*.

Your Java source code files could contain more than one class declaration or implementation. In this case, *javac* creates a bytecode binary object for each class and stores it in a separate file with the .class extension.

For instance, if your Java source code file declares three new classes called **NewClassA**, **NewClassB**, and **NewClassC** in a file named NewClassA.java, *javac* would create three new files, NewClassA.class, NewClassB.class, and NewClassC.class. These three new classes are created in the same directory as the source code files unless the -d command-line option is specified when invoking *javac*. If this command-line switch is invoked, the default is overridden by the directory you specify.

If a referenced class doesn't exist in the source code file when compiling several classes, *javac* searches for this class based upon the values specified within the CLASSPATH environment variable. If the referenced class is not found in either the source code file or in the class path, a compile-time exception occurs and an error message is generated.

javac_g

A nonoptimizing version of *javac* named *javac_g* is designed to be used with a debugger like *dbx* or *gdb*. Using either of these debuggers is a great idea when you're trying to decipher the sometimes-cryptic compile-time error messages that *javac* issues. This can provide much more information about what's broken and where things start to get weird.

Here's the command for the nonoptimizing compiler:

```
javac_g RenderImageApp.java
```

This produces a binary object that one of the debuggers can use to trace variables and their values, or to step through the execution of your source code. It can even find where the bomb in your code explodes when you reference a class that can't be found!

Compilation Options

Both Java compilers accommodate the same set of command-line options that control the type of bytecode representation the compilation will create. Here they are:

* `-classpath <path>`

This option designates a path in the file system that either compiler uses to find referenced classes. If assigned a value, this option overrides

141

the CLASSPATH environment variable. Directories in <path> are colon-separated paths. The general format for <path> is:

```
.:path1:path2:path3
```

Notice the period that starts this string; it's a context indicator that means the current working directory. Here's an example:

```
javac -classpath .:/home/classes:/export/classes Spam.java
```

- -d <directory>

This option defines the root directory for the class hierarchy. Use this option when you want any resulting compiled class file to be saved in a directory other than the one that contains the source code file. For example:

```
javac -d /home/apps/classes Spam.java
```

In this example, the class file named **Spam.class** is not saved in the same directory as the source code, but rather in the /home/apps/classes directory.

- -g

This option enables the generation of debugging tables necessary for using external debuggers. These tables contain information about variables, methods, and line numbers in the Java source code file. Here's an example:

```
javac -g Spam.java
```

- -ng

This options disables the generation of debugging tables. This creates a smaller bytecode representation of a compiled Java class file but renders the bytecode useless to external debuggers. Use this option only if the -g option is turned on by default in your runtime system. Here's an example:

```
javac -ng Spam.java
```

- -nowarn

This option turns off compiler warnings. If this option is used, the Java compiler sends no compile-time errors to STDERR. Here's an example:

```
javac -nowarn Spam.java
```

- -O

This option optimizes your compiled class. It compiles all static, final, and private methods inline. The danger here is that this could result in a larger bytecode representation of your compiled class; the upside is that the class should execute faster in Java's runtime environment. Which do you prefer: speed or space? Here's an example:

```
javac -O Spam.java
```

- -verbose

This option instructs the compiler and linker to echo all compile and link messages to STDERR. These messages contain information about all the Java source files compiled and classes loaded. Here's an example:

```
javac -verbose Spam.java
```

This produces the following sample output, echoed to SDTERR:

```
[parsed Spam.java in 2352ms]
[checking class Spam]
[loaded /html/classes/browser/Applet.class in 813ms]
[loaded /html/classes/java/lang/Object.class in 124ms]
[loaded /html/classes/awt/Graphics.class in 461ms]
[wrote Spam.class]
[done in 9479ms]
```

Verbose, indeed!

Installing Java Applications

After you successfully compile a new application, you need to define a location for that application and its associated compiled classes. In some cases, this may be in a well-known directory already defined in your CLASSPATH environment variable. In other cases (like when you're testing code that's not yet ready for prime time), the location may be new and private. In this case, you need to append the new location onto your CLASSPATH environment variable.

The environment variable CLASSPATH is specified by a colon-separated list of directories. These directories list the locations for bytecode representations of compiled classes in your run-time system.

Here's an example of a UNIX C shell definition of CLASSPATH:

```
setenv CLASSPATH .:/html/classes:/export/system/classes
```

In this example, three locations are specified. First, the initial dot defines the current working directory. The second directory designates that compiled classes may also be found in the directory /html/classes. The final entry specifies that compiled classes also may be found in the directory named /export/system/classes.

The Java runtime system does some extra manipulation of the CLASS-PATH variable. It always appends the location of the system classes onto the current value of the CLASSPATH environment variable unless the -classpath option is used. This option provides an alternate location for the system classes.

If you look at the HotJava executable in your distribution, you see that it's really a wrapper script, not a binary file. Such scripts are valuable because they provide a much simpler user interface to Java applications while providing complex set-up and execution options to the Java runtime system.

For instance, in the hotjava/bin directory of the Alpha2 distribution, the wrapper is a Korn shell script named .java_wrapper. This script sets several environment variables, determines the proper architecture of the binary to execute, and finally executes the program in the Java runtime system on the file or files specified on the command line. In fact, this wrapper is used for all these programs: *hotjava*, *java*, *javac*, *javadoc*, *javah*, *javap*, and *javaprof*.

It's a good idea to create a wrapper script for your new Java applications. This allows you to manage where their compiled classes are stored and how they're referenced by users. You can then install this wrapper script in your common tools directory so other users can begin to use your new applications.

Step-by-Step Compilation & Installation

In this section, we guide you through each step of compiling and installing the RenderImageApp application you created in the previous chapter. In this section, you also create a wrapper script for RenderImageApp.

Step 1: Compile RenderImageApp.java

In this step, you compile the Java source code file named RenderImageApp.java in the /html/classes directory. You should invoke the Java compiler with the -g option to enable debugging table generation and the -verbose option to echo compiler and loader information. On the command line, enter:

```
javac -g -verbose RenderImageApp.java
```

A successful compilation results in neither warnings nor compilation error messages, while class files RenderImageApp.class, renderWindow.class, inputWindow.class, and urlField.class are created in the /html/classes directory.

Compilation warnings may result in an interpretable class, but the resulting bytecode cannot be considered safe. One exception to this rule occurs when your code contains dusty corners of code that may never be reached by the execution thread. For example, the implementation of the system class named NetworkServer contains a *while* loop that never terminates unless the process is explicitly killed. The next line after this *while* block is a *close( )* statement.

The Java compiler prints a warning message that this statement is never reached. This is not harmful, and the compiled class can be considered safe for execution. That is, execution will not result in any undesired side effects that could wreak havoc on your local system.

An unsuccessful compile results in compilation error messages. These messages are verbose, and provide considerable information about the problem and where in the source code file it originates. For example, the compilation of a Java source code file named TC.java resulted in the following error messages:

```
chevelle:/html/classes[] javac TC.java
TC.java:48: Class tc not found in type declaration.
        public void ReadObj(tc tcnew) {
                    ^
TC.java:49: Undefined variable: tcNew
        inObject = tcNew;
                   ^

2 errors
```

Each error message lists the file name, the line number in the source code, and an explanation of the error. In the preceding example, the first error occurs in the TC.java file on line 48. The compiler couldn't find the class tc referenced in the argument list of the method named ReadObj. The second error message is related to the first; it's in the same file, but on line 49. The compiler found an undefined variable because the argument list for the method on line 48 specified an incorrect variable name (**tcNew** instead of **tcnew**).

Continue with this step until all errors are fixed. It's the only way your code has a chance of working properly!

Step 2: Recompile for Optimization

In this step, you recompile the RenderImageApp application for optimization and to disable debugger table generation. On the command line, enter:

```
javac -O -ng -verbose RenderImageApp.java
```

This creates an optimized bytecode representation for the RenderImageApp application. It also disables the creation of debugging tables, which increase the size of the resulting bytecode class file. (Note: The -ng option may not be necessary; it depends whether your site enables debugging table generation as a default.)

Step 3: Write a UNIX Wrapper Script

In this step, you write a wrapper script that provides a simple interface to the RenderImageApp application. In this script, several site-independent environment variables are set; alter these lines of the script accordingly.

This script can become a template for similar scripts for all the Java applications you develop. All you need to do is alter the application location and name in the script. You might also need to adjust the class path to include specific classes required to run your applications. You might also add additional options to the Java interpreter, if you desire.

In your text editor, enter this Bourne shell wrapper script for the RenderImageApp application:

```
#!/bin/sh

# Set the required HotJava home environment variable
export HOTJAVA_HOME
if [ -z "$HOTJAVA_HOME" ].
then
    echo "Please set your HOTJAVA_HOME environment variable."
    exit
fi
```

```
# Set the class path environment variable
export CLASSPATH
if [ -z "$CLASSPATH" ]
then
     CLASSPATH="."
fi


# *********** Modify the value of this variable *****************
# Set the application directory in which the bytecode class
# files are found
appdir=/html/classes/



# *********** Modify the value of this variable*****************
# If the location of your application is not found in your current
# class path, either change your CLASSPATH environment variable
# or append the location to this shell environment variable. The
# latter method makes the change to this variable local in scope.
# Outside this shell, this variable reverts back to its original
# value.
CLASSPATH="$CLASSPATH:$HOTJAVA_HOME/classes:$appdir"



# *********** Modify the value of this variable*****************
# Set the name of the application
app=RenderImageApp

if [ ! -d "$appdir" ]
then
    echo "Unable to change to the application directory $appdir"
    exit
else
    cd "$appdir"
fi


# Set the options for the Java interpreter
# The -classpath option instructs the interpreter
# where to look for classes.
```

```
opts='-classpath "$CLASSPATH"'

# Set the absolute path to the java interpreter
prog=$HOTJAVA_HOME/bin/java

# Everything up to this point is optional, but helps to maintain
# a nice, orderly environment--which is why we use it ourselves

if [ -f "$prog" ]
then
    eval exec $prog $opts $app
else
    echo "Could not find the java interpreter."
    exit
fi
```

Step 4: Save the Script

In this step, save the Bourne shell script as a hidden file named .render_image_app_wrapper in a place in your file system where other scripts are located. We suggest /usr/local/bin for most UNIX implementations. Therefore, the absolute name of the wrapper script is /usr/local/bin/.render_image_app_wrapper. Why a hidden file, you ask? So when your users list the directory, the script won't be visible. If they don't know it's there, they'll be less likely to change it.

Step 5: Install the Wrapper Script

Here, you install the wrapper script and make a symbolic link from RenderImage to that script. The link is meant to simplify invocation of the RenderImageApp application. First, change to the /usr/local/bin directory. (You need at least write permission for this directory.) If you don't have the proper permissions, contact your site's system administrator.

On the command line, enter (or have the administrator enter):

```
ln -s .render_image_app_wrapper RenderImage
```

This creates a symbolic link named RenderImage in the /usr/local/bin directory. To invoke the RenderImageApp, enter the following on the command line:

```
RenderImage &
```

This implicitly runs the wrapper script, sets the correct environment variable, and invokes the Java interpreter on the RenderImageApp application. Users can invoke RenderImage anywhere in the file system if /usr/local/bin is on their path.

csh and tcsh Users Only!
You need to rehash the shell so it can find the new script!

Step 6: Test Your New Application

In this step, you test your new RenderImageApp application. Remember, the command-line interface to this application is named RenderImage. This is the command your users will invoke, rather than the more obscure command RenderImageApp, which is the name of the controlling class for your new Java application.

To test the new application, change to your home directory and enter the following on the command line:

```
RenderImage &
```

If the shell returns an error message that the command cannot be found, check the permissions for the wrapper script. The permissions on .render_image_app_wrapper should be executable by world, group, and user for UNIX implementations. If the shell returns an error message that the RenderImageApp class cannot be found, check your CLASSPATH environment variable. You could have entered the application's directory incorrectly.

Now, test the new application by specifying the URL of an initial image to render in the renderWindow canvas. For this example, we assume you have a .GIF image in your file system named /html/images/warning.gif. So, on the command line enter:

```
RenderImage file:/html/images/warning.gif &
```

This invocation should load warning.gif onto the canvas of the renderWindow of the RenderImageApp application.

Summary

Java's extensibility and reusability require careful management and organization. The design and installation of a class library should result from an intense and thorough process of analysis and consideration of existing classes, methods, and constructors.

The Java compiler offers numerous command-line options to control source code handling. Installation of Java applications can be greatly simplified by creating a wrapper script to control the required environment and provide a simple execution interface. Finally, wrapper scripts should be installed in well-known or common system locations.

In the next chapter, you learn how to take an existing Java application and extend its capabilities in much the same way that you learned how to extend Java applets in Chapter 5.

## CHAPTER 8

Extending Java

Applications

a Java application can be easily extended in much the same
fashion as its sibling, the Java applet. In this chapter, we present a new Java application named NetLogger written by F.
Sid Conklin from Stanford University. NetLogger listens on a user- or
server-provided port on a UNIX machine and reports any connections
to that port to the user via STDOUT.

NetLogger is an extension of the system class named **NetworkServer**,
a new addition to the Java Alpha3 distribution. **NetLogger** is a simple,
easy-to-understand implementation of a server built using Java. It is run
from a command line in a shell, in which it reports to STDOUT.

In this chapter, we present an extension of **NetLogger** called
WinNetLogger that reports connection status information to STDOUT
and writes messages to a text window with vertical and horizontal
scrollbars.

Extending an Application

In this section, we present an existing Java application called NetLogger, an extension of that program called WinNetLogger, and a Java class named **NetworkServer**.

NetLogger Application

Sid Conklin graciously provided the NetLogger application for use in this book. NetLogger starts a server on a specified port of a UNIX machine. By default, the port ID is set to 8888 by the NetworkServer class, but the ID can also be specified via the command line.

After the server begins listening on a port, it also begins echoing client messages sent to the server on that port to the STDOUT file handle of a UNIX machine. NetLogger is a useful example of the ease of use and the power inherent in the Java programming language.

Here's the NetLogger specification:

```
/*
 * NetLogger
 *
 * Based on Middleware, NetLogger opens listening ports to receive
 * log message from various log/trace servers.
 *
 * @version1.0, 27 July 1995
 * @authorF. Sid Conklin
 */

import net.*;
import java.io.*;
import java.lang.*;

public class NetLogger extends NetworkServer{

    /* Constants declaration */
    final    int      kMaxBuffSize    = 256;


    public NetLogger (){

      /* Nothing really needs to happen here. If we were using the
```

Middleware Service Broker we would make a call to determine
the Event Brokers socket, then send a subscription event to
Event Broker. Event Broker would then inform all log/trace servers
that this application is interested in certain events */

```java
/* Debug Message */
System.out.println("NetLogger Constructor");
}


/* Main method invoked at runtime */
public static void main(String args[]) {
    Integer port = null;
    NetLogger Listener = null;

    if (args.length > 0)
    {
        /* if the user enters input, it should be the port number */
        port = new Integer(args[0]);
        new NetLogger().startServer(port.intValue());


    }
    else
      {
        port = new Integer(new NetLogger().startServer());
        /*In the alpha3 code that our tech editor used, the
        NetworkServer.startServer method is void (doesn't return an
        int), and it requires an integer passed into it as a
        parameter. So he had to make the above, single line of Java
        code into the following 2 lines:
        port = new Integer( 8888 );
        new NetLogger().startServer( 8888 );
        to get it to compile and run. If your version of the
        NetworkServer class is like his, you'll need to make these
        changes. He noticed from the code below that there are two
        methods--one that takes an int parameter and one that
        doesn't--but his version's code didn't have two methods. You
        should take appropriate corrective action! */

      }
```

```
    /* Tell users what port we are listening on */
    System.out.println("port: "+ port.toString());
  }


  /* This method is called when a client attaches to a listening
  port. The following method overshadows the
  NetworkServer.serviceRequest method */
  public void serviceRequest() {

    byte buf[] = new byte[kMaxBuffSize]; // Maximum buffer read
    String logMessage;
    int logMessSize;

    /* Read from client stream and load buffer */
    logMessSize = clientInput.read(buf,0,buf.length);

    /* Convert buffer to string for output */
    logMessage = neString(buf,0,0,logMessSize);

    /* Dump to Standard Out */
    System.out.println(logMessage);
  }
}
```

net.NetworkServer Class Specification

This is included to complete the example application presented in this chapter. The **NetworkServer** class appears in the Alpha3 distribution in a similar form. All differences are explained later in this chapter.

In the following specification, Conklin has added a new method named **startServer**, and has passed this onto Sun Microsystems for integration into a future system class library. Here's the source for NetworkServer.java:

```
/*
 * @(#)NetworkServer.java1.4 95/05/11 James Gosling
 *
 * Copyright (c) 1994 Sun Microsystems, Inc. All Rights Reserved.
 *
```

```
 * Permission to use, copy, modify, and distribute this software and
 * its documentation for NON-COMMERCIAL purposes and without fee is
 * hereby granted provided that this copyright notice appears in all
 * copies. Please refer to the file "copyright.html" for further
 * important copyright and licensing information.
 *
 * SUN MAKES NO REPRESENTATIONS OR WARRANTIES ABOUT THE SUITABILITY
 * OF THE SOFTWARE, EITHER EXPRESS OR IMPLIED, INCLUDING BUT NOT
 * LIMITED TO THE IMPLIED WARRANTIES OF MERCHANTABILITY, FITNESS FOR
 * A PARTICULAR PURPOSE, OR NON-INFRINGEMENT. SUN SHALL NOT BE
 * LIABLE FOR ANY DAMAGES SUFFERED BY LICENSEE AS A RESULT OF USING,
 * MODIFYING OR DISTRIBUTING THIS SOFTWARE OR ITS DERIVATIVES.
 *
 * Revision History
 *
 *   Author              Date            Comments
 *   F. Sid Conklin      7/27/95         Added startServer() method
 *
 */
package net;

import net.*;
import java.io.*;

/**
 * This is the base class for network servers. To define a new type
 * of server define a new subclass of NetworkServer with a
 * serviceRequest method that services one request. Start the server
 * by executing:
 * <pre>
 * new MyServerClass().startServer(port);
 * </pre>
 */
public class NetworkServer implements Runnable {

  /** Socket for communicating with client. */
  public Socket clientSocket = null;
  private Thread serverInstance;
  private boolean isServer;
```

```
/** Stream for printing to the client. */
public PrintStream clientOutput;

/** Buffered stream for reading replies from client. */
public InputStream clientInput;

/** Close an open connection to the client. */
public void close() {
        try {
                clientOutput.close();
        } catch(Exception e) {}
        try {
                clientInput.close();
        } catch(Exception e) {}
        try {
                clientSocket.close();
        } catch(Exception e) {}

        clientSocket = null;
        clientInput = null;
        clientOutput = null;
}


/** Return client connection status */
public boolean clientIsOpen() {
        return clientSocket != null;
}


final public void run() {
        if (isServer) {
            Thread.currentThread().setPriority(Thread.MAX_PRIORITY);
            System.out.print("Server starts " + clientSocket + "\n");

            while (true) {
                try {
                    Socket ns = clientSocket.accept();
                    System.out.print("New connection " + ns + "\n");
                    NetworkServer n = (NetworkServer) clone();
```

```
                        n.clientSocket = ns;
                        n.isServer = false;
                        new Thread(n).start();
                    } catch(Exception e) {
                        System.out.print("Server failure\n");
                        e.printStackTrace();
                        clientSocket.close();
                        System.out.print("cs="+clientSocket.port+"\n");
                        System.out.print("ia="+clientSocket.address+"\n");
                        Socket nns = new Socket(true);
                        nns.port = clientSocket.port;
                        nns.bindToPort(clientSocket.address,
                                          clientSocket.port);
                        clientSocket = nns;
                    }
            } else {
                    try {
                            clientOutput = new PrintStream(
                            new BufferedOutputStream(
                                    clientSocket.outputStream), false);
                            clientInput =
                                    new BufferedInputStream(
                                            clientSocket.inputStream);
                            serviceRequest();
                            System.out.print(
                                "Service handler exits"+clientSocket+"\n");
                    } catch(Exception e) {
                            System.out.print("Service handler failure\n");
                            // e.printStackTrace();
                    }
                    close();
                }
        }

/** Start a server on port <i>port</i>.  It will call
 * serviceRequest() for each new connection. */
final public void startServer(int port) {
```

```
        Socket s = new Socket(true);
        InetAddress addr = InetAddress.getByName(
                InetAddress.localHostName);
        int I;

        for (i = 10; —i >= 0;) {
                try {
                   s.port = port;
                   s.bindToPort(addr, port);
                   break;
                } catch(Exception e) {
                   System.out.print("[Waiting to create port]\n");
                   Thread.sleep(5000);
                }
        }

        if (i < 0) {
           System.out.print("**Failed to create port\n");
           return;
        }

        s.listen(50);
        serverInstance = new Thread(this);
        isServer = true;
        clientSocket = s;
        serverInstance.start();
}


/** Start a server on Anonymous port. It will call
 * serviceRequest() for each new connection.*/
public int startServer() {

        Socket s = new Socket(true);
        InetAddress addr = InetAddress.getByName(
                InetAddress.localHostName);

        /* Let the server pick an un-used port to Listen on */
        s.bindAnonymously(addr);
```

158

```
        /* Debug */
        System.out.println("Debug: Listening Port-> " + s.port );

        /* Start Listening connection depth of 50 */
        s.listen(50);

        serverInstance = neThread(this);
        isServer = true;
        clientSocket = s;
        serverInstance.start();

        return s.port;
    }


/** Service one request. It is invoked with the clientInput and
* clientOutput streams initialized.  This method handles one
* client connection. When it is done, it can simply exit. The
* default server just echoes its input. It is invoked in its own
* private thread. */
public void serviceRequest() {

        byte buf[] = new byte[300];
        int n;

        clientOutput.print(
                "Echo server " + getClass().getName() + "\n");
        clientOutput.flush();

        while ((n = clientInput.read(buf, 0, buf.length)) >= 0) {
                clientOutput.write(buf, 0, n);
        }
    }


public static void main(String argv[]) {
        new NetworkServer ().startServer(8888);
    }


public NetworkServer () {}
}
```

Step-by-Step Extension & Installation

In this section, we guide you through a step-by-step extension of NetLogger. The extension is called **WinNetLogger**. **WinNetLogger** has the same functionality as NetLogger. The only difference is that instead of reporting client messages to STDOUT, it writes messages to a window with scrollbars.

Step 1: Create a File Named WinNetLogger.java and Import Required System Packages

In this step, create a file named WinNetLogger.java to contain a new extension to the **NetLogger** class with your text editor. Next, import the required system packages and classes for the new **WinNetLogger** class. In your file, enter this code:

```
import net.*;
import java.io.*;
import java.lang.*;
import awt.*;
```

The **net** package contains classes and methods to handle socket manipulation. The **java.io** package contains basic input and output methods. **java.lang** contains basic language constructs support such as integer and string. Finally, the **awt** packages contain classes and methods for dealing with windows.

Step 2: Declare the WinNetLogger Class

In this step, you insert the **WinNetLogger** class declaration into the Java source code file named WinNetLogger.java. Following the import statements, enter this code:

```
public class WinNetLogger extends NetLogger {
    ... body of class ...
}
```

This creates a public class named **WinNetLogger** as an extension to the **NetLogger** class. **NetLogger** is not a member of the system library of classes, so it must appear in the same directory as the

WinNetLogger class. Otherwise, its home directory must be defined in the CLASSPATH environment variable that the Java interpreter uses to search for referenced classes.

Step 3: Declare Class Variables

In this step, you declare necessary class variables. Within the body of the **WinNetLogger** class, enter this code:

```
// Declare class variables for WinNetLogger class
static StatusWindow sw = null; // status window display canvas
static WServer server = null; // current window server
```

The sw class variable is where a port's messages are rendered. This is a frame that contains a **TextArea** widget where messages will accumulate as they're received at the server's specified port. The server class variable is the name of the current window server required for window-typed Java applications.

Step 4: Declare and Implement the WinNetLogger Constructor

In this step, you code the **WinNetLogger** public constructor. It takes no arguments. After the class variable declarations, enter this code:

```
// Declare constructor for WinNetLogger class
public WinNetLogger() {
     super();
}
```

All this constructor does is call the constructor for the superclass named **NetLogger.** This prints the string "NetLogger Constructor" to the shell that invoked the application.

Step 5: Declare and Implement the Main Method

In this step, you create the main method for the **WinNetLogger** Java application. This method is required for all stand-alone Java applications. Please notice that this main method overrides the main method for the superclass **NetLogger.** Enter the following method information immediately following the constructor declaration:

```
/* This is the main method of the WinNetLogger class and controls
 * execution of the WinNetLogger application. It takes as
 * arguments command-line input stored in the args array. */
public static void main(String args[]) {
  Integer port = null; // port number of server
  WinNetLogger Listner = null; // port sniffer

  // Create a new window server and start it.
  server = new WServer();
  server.start();

    /* Create a new status window frame. This is the parent
     * object of the TextArea window where messages received by
     * the server are echoed to the user. This differs from the
     * NetLogger class, which echos the messages to STDOUT. */
    sw = n neStatusWindow(server);

    /* Decide if the user specified a port to listen to. The
     * default port number is 8888, which is specified in the
     * NetworkServer class specification. */
    if(args.length > 0) {
      port = new Integer(args[0]); // port specified by user

      // Create new object and start the server
      new WinNetLogger().startServer(port.intValue());
    }
    else {
      /* Default port specified--none specified on the
       * command line by the user. */
      port = new Integer(new WinNetLogger().startServer());
    }
}
```

Step 6: Declare and Implement the serviceRequest Method

In this step, you create a required method named **serviceRequest.** This method overrides the serviceRequest method for the **NetworkServer** system class. You must use this exact name for this method, which services a single request from a client for the current **NetworkServer** that is an instance of the **WinNetLogger** class.

After the main method declaration, enter this code:

```
/* This method services one request. It works with the
 * 'clientInput' and 'clientOuput' data streams of the
 * NetworkServer class. This method reads a message from a buffer
 * and then assigns it to a class variable of the
 * StatusWindow class named 'sw'. In the end, this message string is
 * written to the TextArea display window of the WinNetLogger
 * application. This method takes no arguments. */
public void serviceRequest() {

  /* Create buffer to hold message. The size of the array
   * is kMaxBuffSize, which is a static class variable of
   * NetLogger. */
  byte buf[] = new byte[kMaxBuffSize];

  // Declare local variables
  String logMessage; // message string
  int logMessSize;   // length of message

 /* Determine the length of the message. 'clientInput' is
  * an InputStream type object from the NetworkServer
  * class and it is a buffered stream used for reading
  * replies from connected clients. 'clientInput.read' is
  * a public method of the InputStream system class and
  * it reads a certain number of bytes from a named buffer. */
  logMessSize = clientInput.read(buf,0,buf.length);

  // Create a new string to hold the message
  logMessage = neString(buf,0,0,logMessSize);

  /* Assign the = nemessage to the 'sw' class variable using a
   * public method of the StatusWindow class named sw.setMessage.*/
  sw.setMessage(logMessage);
}
```

Note: At the end of this chapter, you'll find the entire specification for the **WinNetLogger** class.

Step 7: Declare and Implement the StatusWindow Class

In this step, you create a new class named **StatusWindow**. This is the base window object for the **WinNetLogger** application. This frame object is runnable, which means that it executes continuously, and updates the list of messages received by a **NetworkServer** server. This class uses the **Runnable** interface to permit it to operate in this fashion.

After the **WinNetLogger** class code, enter this code for the **StatusWindow** class:

```
/* This is the StatusWindow class declaration and
 * implementation. This class is an extension of a system class
 * named Frame and implements the Runnable interface. This
 * allows the StatusWindow class to continually update its
 * information. */
class StatusWindow extends Frame implements Runnable {

  // Declare instance variables
  public int position; // current position in the TextArea display
  TextArea t; // TextArea widget to display messages
  Font font; // Font used to render messages in TextArea canvas

  /* Declare and implement the constructor, which takes the
   * current window server as its only argument. */
  public StatusWindow(WServer server) {

    /* Call the constructor of the Frame superclass. It
     *  takes as arguments: the current window server, it has a
     * title bar, it has no parent frame, it is 400 pixels wide and
     * 400 pixels high, and it has a light-gray color background. */
    super(server,true,null,400,400,Color.lightGray);

    /* Get the font from the current window server. wServer is a
     * public instance variable of the awt.Container system package.
     * wServer.fonts is an instance variable of type FontTable.
     * wServer.fonts.getFont is a public method of a FontTable
     * object.*/
    font = wServer.fonts.getFont("Helvetica",Font.PLAIN,16);
```

```
// Set the title of the display window
setTitle("WinNetLogger");

/* Create a new element of the parent frame object StatusWindow.
 * This new element is a Window type object and is created
 * with: the current frame object as its parent, the name of the
 * orientation of the new window, the background of the parent
 * frame, and the parent frame's width and height. */
Window w = n neWindow(this,"Center",background,width,height);

/* Set the layout of this window element of the parent frame
 * into columns. */
w.setLayout(new ColumnLayout(true));

/* Create a new element of the current Window object with: the
 * current window, orientation specification, the font, width,
 * and height of the parent frame. */
t = new TextArea(w,"Center",font,width,height);

/* Set the horizontal and vertical fill and make the text set
 * into the TextArea noneditable. */
t.setHFill(true);
t.setVFill(true);
t.setEditable(false);

/* Initialize the current position to start writing messages
 * into the TextArea. */
position = 0;

// Map the new elements into the StatusWindow frame.
map();

// Resize the new frame and its Window and TextArea elements.
resize();

/* Start a new thread for the Runnable interface of the
 * StatusWindow frame.*/
= neThread(this).start();
}
```

Step 8: Declare and Implement the run Method

In this step, you create the run method required for all Java **Runnable** interfaces. This begins execution of the **Runnable** interface for the **StatusWindow** frame. After the **StatusWindow** constructor, enter this code:

```
/* This is the method to run the Runnable interface of the
 * StatusWindow frame object. */
public void run() {
    setMessage("Starting server log ...\n\n");
}
```

Step 9: Declare and Implement the setMessage Method

In this step, you create the **setMessage** method for the **StatusWindow** class. This method inserts a message received from the client by the server into the display window. After the run method, add this code:

```
/* This method sets the message received by the server from the
 * client into a TextArea starting at the specified position.*/
public void setMessage(String message) {

  // Insert the current message at the current position
  t.insertText(message,position);

  // Increment the current position.
  position += message.length();
}
```

Note: At the end of this chapter, you'll find the complete **StatusWindow** class code.

Step 10: Save WinNetLogger.java

In this step, save the Java source code you just entered as a file named WinNetLogger.java.

Step 11: Create a File Named NetworkServer.java

In this step, you may need to create a Java source code file in the /html/classes directory named NetworkServer.java. Consult the sidebar for details.

Which Java Alpha Version Are You Using?

If you have a new HotJava/Java distribution (Alpha3 or later), you can skip Step 11 if the system class NetworkServer.java already includes a defined method named startServer. To check this, find the class sources directory, typically <my_path>/hotjava/classsrc/net/, for the net package in your distribution directory. If a Java source file named NetworkServer.java exists in this directory, view it with an editor and search for the string startServer, or use the following UNIX search command:

```
grep startServer NetworkServer.java
```

If the **startServer** method is defined, skip this step. If it isn't, you need to create a local copy of the WindowServer.java file in the /html/classes directory.

You can do this either by entering the code that follows later in this section or by copying WindowServer.java from the system library (if this file exists). If you can copy the file, all you need to do is to add the **startServer** method.

These convoluted efforts result from Java's alpha release status. We want your experience with Java to be filled with the newest and most useful methods and classes; unfortunately, this sometimes requires extra work on your part.

The source code for the local copy of NetworkServer.java file is defined earlier in this chapter in the section entitled net.NetworkServer Class Specification. Enter this code and save the file as NetworkServer.java. (Note: You may have a version of the code that has only one **startServer** method rather than two. If so, consult the comment about changing the code in the NetLogger listing at the beginning of this chapter.)

Step 12: Save NetworkServer.java and Compile the NetworkServer Class

After ensuring that NetworkServer.java resides on your local hard disk in the /html/classes directory, compile the new **NetworkServer** class into a class file named NetworkServer.class in the /html/classes directory (i.e., the same directory as the source file). Finally, change to the /html/classes directory and enter the following on the command line:

```
javac -verbose NetworkServer.java
```

If this compile fails, fix the errors and recompile.

Note: This step is only necessary if you didn't already have the **NetworkServer** class installed on your system, i.e., if you also had to perform step 11.

Step 13: Compile the NetLogger Class

In this step, you compile the new **NetLogger** class into a class file named NetLogger.class in the /html/classes directory—again, the same directory as the source file. Change to the /html/classes directory and enter the following on the command line:

```
javac -verbose NetLogger.java
```

If this compile fails, fix the errors and recompile.

Step 14: Compile the WinNetLogger Class

In this step, you compile the new **WinNetLogger** class into a class file named WinNetLogger.class in the /html/classes directory—the same directory as the source file. Change to the /html/classes directory and enter the following on the command line:

```
javac -verbose WinNetLogger.java
```

If this compile fails, fix the errors and recompile.

Step 15: Create a UNIX Wrapper Script

In this step, you get a chance to recover from the repetition of the last three steps. Here, you write a wrapper script that provides a simple interface to the WinNetLogger application. In this script, several site-dependent environment variables are set. You should alter these lines of the script accordingly.

In your text editor, enter this Bourne shell wrapper script for the WinNetLogger application:

```
#!/bin/sh
# Set the required HotJava home environment variable.
export HOTJAVA_HOME
if [ -z "$HOTJAVA_HOME" ]
then
    echo "Please set your HOTJAVA_HOME environment variable."
    exit
fi
```

```sh
# Set the class path environment variable
export CLASSPATH
if [ -z "$CLASSPATH" ]
then
     CLASSPATH="."
fi


# Include the system class library
export LD_LIBRARY_PATH
LD_LIBRARY_PATH="$LD_LIBRARY_PATH:$HOTJAVA_HOME/lib"


# *********** Modify the value of this variable *****************
# Set the application directory where the bytecode class files are
# found.
appdir=/html/classes/



# *********** Modify the value of this variable*****************
# If the location of your application is not found in your current
# class path, either change your CLASSPATH environment variable
# or append the location to this shell environment variable. The
# later method makes the change to this variable local in scope.
# Outside this shell, this variable reverts back to its original
# value.
CLASSPATH="$CLASSPATH:$HOTJAVA_HOME/classes:$appdir"



# *********** Modify the value of this variable*****************
# Set the name of the application
app=WinNetLogger

if [ ! -d "$appdir" ]
then
    echo "Unable to change to the application directory $appdir"
    exit
else
    cd "$appdir"
fi
```

169

```
# Set the options for the Java interpreter
# The -classpath option instructs the interpreter
# where to look for classes.
opts='-classpath "$CLASSPATH"'

# Set the absolute path to the java interpreter
prog=$HOTJAVA_HOME/bin/java

if [ -f "$prog" ]
then
    eval exec $prog $opts $app '$@'
else
    echo "Could not find the java interpreter."
    exit
fi
```

Step 16: Save the Script As .winnetlogger_app_wrapper

In this step, you save the Bourne shell script as a hidden file. With your editor, save the preceding script file as .winnetlogger_app_wrapper on your file system in a place where other scripts are located. We suggest /usr/local/bin for most UNIX implementations. Therefore, the absolute name of the wrapper script is: /usr/local/bin/.winnetlogger_app_wrapper.

Why a hidden file? That keeps the script invisible. So when your users list that directory, they can't see it and probably won't try to change it. In real life, you'll probably want to restrict the elements in /usr/local/bin to production applications; for the experiments in this book, you'll probably want to use another (and more private) directory.

Step 17: Install the Script

In this step, you make a symbolic link from WinNetLogger to the wrapper script. This link simplifies the invocation of the WinNetLogger application. First, change to the /usr/local/bin directory (or whatever private directory you're using). You'll need at least write permission for this directory; if you don't have the proper permission, contact your system administrator.

On the command line, enter:

```
ln -s .winnetlogger_app_wrapper WinNetLogger
```

This creates a symbolic link named WinNetLogger in the /usr/local/bin directory. To invoke the WinNetLogger and make it listen to port 8080, enter the following on the command line:

```
WinNetLogger 8080 &
```

This implicitly runs the wrapper script, sets the correct environment variable, and invokes the Java interpreter for the WinNetLogger application. Users can invoke WinNetLogger anywhere in the file system if /usr/local/bin is in their shell path.

For csh and tcsh Users Only

csh and *tcsh* users need to rehash the shell so it can find the new script.

Step 18: Test the WinNetLogger Application

In this step, you use telnet to test your new application. telnet can be directed to connect to a specific port, so you use telnet to act as a client to connect to port 8080 on the machine that's running your new WinNetLogger application and its bundled server, a **NetworkServer** object.

For the first test, we assume that the machine that's running WinNetLogger is named chevelle. Of course, you need to substitute the name of the real machine that's running your copy of WinNetLogger.

Enter the following input on the command line in the shell that invoked the WinNetLogger application:

```
telnet chevelle 8080
```

You should see something similar to this:

```
chevelle:/u/bowtie[] telnet chevelle 8080
Trying 148.57.165.16 ...
Connected to chevelle.hal.COM.
Escape character is '^]'.
```

Now, telnet stops and waits for your instructions. For this example, enter this phrase:

```
Java is a great language!
```

This does two things:

1. this phrase is written to your WinNetLogger **TextArea** window; and
2. it terminates the telnet session.

Now, try the same exercise, but from another machine on your network. Again, telnet back to the machine onto port 8080 and enter this phrase:

```
It's fun too.
```

You should see this phrase written to the **TextArea** window on the line below the first phrase. Additional messages received by the server will be appended to the previous messages in the **TextArea** canvas. As long as the server is running, it will report any messages sent by a client to port 8080.

Figure 8-1 shows a screen capture of WinNetLogger with our messages.

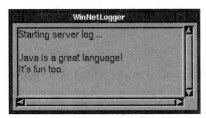

Figure 8-1: The WinNetLogger screen displaying our text

WinNetLogger Specification

Here's the complete WinNetLogger specification. It includes the complete StatusWindow class code referenced earlier in this chapter.

```
import net.*;
import java.io.*;
import java.lang.*;
import awt.*;

public class WinNetLogger extends NetLogger {
// Declare class variables for WinNetLogger class
static StatusWindow sw = null; // status window display canvas
static WServer server = null; // current window server

// Declare constructor for WinNetLogger class
public WinNetLogger() {
  super();
}

/* This is the main method of the WinNetLogger class. It controls
```

```
 * execution of the WinNetLogger application. It takes as arguments
 * command line input stored in the args array. */
public static void main(String args[]) {
  Integer port = null; // port number of server
  WinNetLogger Listner = null; // port sniffer

  // Create a new window server and start it.
  server = new WServer();
  server.start();

  /* Create a new status window frame. This is the parent
   * object of the TextArea window where messages received by
   * the server are echoed to the user. This differs from the
   * NetLogger class, which echos the messages to STDOUT. */
  sw = n neStatusWindow(server);

  /* Decide if the user specified a port to listen to. The default
   * port number is 8888 specified in the NetworkServer class
   * specification. */
  if(args.length > 0) {
    port = new Integer(args[0]); // port specified by user

    // Create new object and start the server
    new WinNetLogger().startServer(port.intValue());
  }
  else {
    /* Default port specified--none specified on the command line
     * by the user. */
    port = new Integer(new WinNetLogger().startServer());
  }
}


/* This method services one request. It works with the 'clientInput'
 * and 'clientOuput' data streams of the NetworkServer class. This
 * method reads a message from a buffer and then assigns it to a
 * class variable of the StatusWindow class named sw. In the end,
 * this message string is written to the TextArea display window of
 * the WinNetLogger application. This method takes no arguments. */
public void serviceRequest() {

  /* Create buffer to hold message. The size of the array is
```

```
      * kMaxBuffSize, which is a static class variable of NetLogger. */
     byte buf[] = new byte[kMaxBuffSize];

     // Declare local variables
     String logMessage; // message string
     int logMessSize;   // length of message

     /* Determine the length of the message. 'clientInput' is an
      * InputStream type object from the NetworkServer class and it is
      * a buffered stream used for reading replies from connected
      * clients. 'clientInput.read' is a public method of the
      * InputStream system class and it reads a certain number of bytes
      * from a named buffer. */
     logMessSize = clientInput.read(buf,0,buf.length);

     // Create a new string to hold the message
     logMessage = neString(buf,0,0,logMessSize);

     /* Assign the = nemessage to the 'sw' class variable using a
      * public method of the StatusWindow class named sw.setMessage. */
     sw.setMessage(logMessage);
     }
}


/* This is the StatusWindow class declaration and implementation.
 * This class is an extension of a system class named Frame and it
 * implements the Runnable interface. This allows the StatusWindow
 * class to continually update its information. */
class StatusWindow extends Frame implements Runnable {

  // Declare instance variables
  public int position; // current position in the TextArea display
  TextArea t; // TextArea widget to display messages
  Font font; // Font used to render messages in TextArea canvas

  /* Declare and implement the constructor, which takes the current
   * window server as its only argument. */
  public StatusWindow(WServer server) {

    /* Call the constructor of the Frame superclass. It takes as
```

```
* arguments: the current window server, it has a title bar, it
* has no parent frame, it is 400 pixels wide and 400 pixels
* high, and it has a light-gray color background. */
super(server,true,null,400,400,Color.lightGray);


/* Get the font from the current window server. wServer is a
 * public instance variable of the awt.Container system package.
 * wServer.fonts is an instance variable of type FontTable.
 * wServer.fonts.getFont is a public method of a FontTable
 * object.*/
font = wServer.fonts.getFont("Helvetica",Font.PLAIN,16);


// Set the title of the display window
setTitle("WinNetLogger");


/* Create a new element of the parent frame object StatusWindow.
 * This new element is a Window type object and it is created
 * with: the current frame object as its parent, the name of the
 * orientation of the new window, the background of the parent
 * frame, and the parent frame's width and height. */
Window w = n neWindow(this,"Center",background,width,height);


/* Set the layout of this window element of the parent frame
 * into columns. */
w.setLayout(new ColumnLayout(true));


/* Create a new element of the current Window object with: the
 * current window, orientation specification, the font, width,
 * and height of the parent frame. */
t = new TextArea(w,"Center",font,width,height);


/* Set the horizontal and vertical fill, and make the text set
 * into the TextArea noneditable. */
t.setHFill(true);
t.setVFill(true);
t.setEditable(false);


/* Initialize the current position to start writing messages
 * into the TextArea. */
position = 0;
```

```
    // Map the new elements into the StatusWindow frame.
    map();

    // Resize the new frame, and its Window and TextArea elements.
    resize();

    /* Start a new thread for the Runnable interface of the
     * StatusWindow frame.*/
    = neThread(this).start();
  }

  /* This is the method to run the Runnable interface of the
   * StatusWindow frame object. */
  public void run() {
    setMessage("Starting server log ...\n\n");
  }

  /* This method sets the message received by the server from the
   * client into a TextArea starting at the specified position.*/
  public void setMessage(String message) {

    // Insert the current message at the current position
    t.insertText(message,position);

    // Increment the current position.
    position += message.length();
  }
}
```

Summary

Extending Java applications is similar to extending Java applets. Fundamentally, it's a matter of taking existing functionality and adding new capabilities, or new classes and methods, to provide the needed behavior. For Java applications, this involves redefining the main method for the main class that controls their execution.

In the next chapter, you learn about writing a protocol handler for Java as we define and add a new kind of protocol (and related document type) to the Java runtime environment. This demonstrates just how easy and slick it is to implement one!

## CHAPTER 9

Writing a Java
Protocol
Handler

*Y*ou not only can extend existing applications with Java, but you can also provide mechanisms and capabilities to handle new types of data and protocols. This procedure should be considered an extension of HotJava's data handling rather than a typical extension to functionality and behavior such as you've seen in previous chapters.

A handler is an executable program that controls how input is interpreted, manipulated, and emitted. Although this sounds like just another program, a handler's role in overall system behavior is quite different.

A handler, coupled with the HotJava browser, adds new functionality to that browser. As you will recall from our discussion in Chapter 1, the HotJava browser isn't tied to any specific protocol or set of protocols like more conventional Web browsers are. Because HotJava can handle protocols dynamically, it is superior to other Web browsers. In fact, multiple handlers can be easily integrated with HotJava, and new handlers can even be integrated on the fly at run time, extending the browser's functionality while it's in use!

In this chapter, we present two simple handlers: one controls an atypical Internet protocol for HotJava; the other provides control over the content of a referenced object.

Protocol Handler

A protocol handler can be written in Java and integrated with HotJava. This further extends HotJava's suite of protocols and provides users with new access to information and data. In this section, we present a protocol named **run**, which executes an existing Java class and renders its results in the HotJava browser.

For example, after creating and compiling a Handler Java class, you could enter the following URL into the Document URL window of the HotJava browser:

```
run:HelloWorld
```

This is a valid URL; it simply contains a new protocol specification. What run does is to invoke the Java interpreter for the specified Java class—in this instance, for the HelloWorld applet class. In the sections that follow, we describe how to create such a protocol handler.

Steps in Writing a run Protocol Handler

In this section, you write a simple protocol handler that runs an applet. (Note: This handler doesn't run a Java application.) In the following example, run renders the string "Hello World!" into the HotJava display window. The directories of both the class that the handler runs and the **HelloWorld** class must be in the CLASSPATH environment variable.

Do Exactly What It Says . . .

While the directory structure used in these step-by-step instructions may seem cumbersome and cluttered, it is very important to follow our directions precisely. One complaint about the HotJava alpha distribution is the rigidity of its structure for the class repository. We don't yet know whether this will change in the commercial release. Keep your fingers crossed!

Step 1: Create Directory Structure

In this step, you create several new directories. For this example, assume that the /html/classes directory contains your class repository. This is separate and distinct from the normal system class library directory structure.

HotJava requires that these directory structures descend from a classes directory. The subsequent child directories to **classes**—**net**, **www**, and **protocol**—must appear as named, and must be created as shown in the following steps. The last directory, **run**, must carry the same name as the **run** protocol handler we create in this section.

1. Create a net directory by entering the following on the command line:

```
mkdir /html/classes/net.
```

2. Create a WWW directory by entering the following on the command line:

```
mkdir /html/classes/net/www.
```

3. Create a protocol directory by entering the following on the command line:

```
mkdir /html/classes/net/www/protocol.
```

4. Create a run directory by entering the following on the command line:

```
mkdir /html/classes/net/www/protocol/run.
```

Step 2: Create a File Named Handler.java

In this step, you create a Java source code file named Handler.java with your text editor. This file *must* be in the /html/classes/net/www/protocol/run directory. Therefore, the absolute path to the handler source file is /html/classes/net/www/protocol/run/Handler.java.

Step 3: Declare the net.www.protocol.run Package

In this step, you declare the **net.www.protocol.run** package. This package contains one class named **Handler**. In your text editor, enter this code:

```
// Declare that the following class is part of this package
package net.www.protocol.run
```

Step 4: Import the Required System Packages

In this step, you import the required system packages for the new **Handler** class to function. Enter the following import statements:

```
// Include classes to handle input and output
import java.io.*;
// Include classes to handle HTML document content
import net.www.html.*;
```

179

Step 5: Declare the Handler Class

In this step, you declare the new **Handler** class. Enter this code:

```
// Declare the new run Handler class
class Handler extends URLStreamHandler {
    ... body of class ...
}
```

This new **Handler** class is an extension of the system class named **URLStreamHandler**, which is a member of the **net.www.html** package. Subclasses of the **URLStreamHandler** class provide mechanisms to create data streams for specific types of protocols. In our example, **Handler** handles the new run protocol, and is an extension or a subclass of **URLStreamHandler**.

Step 6: Declare and Implement the openStream Method

In this step, you declare and implement a method named **openStream**. The **URLStreamHandler** class, which is an *abstract* class, also has a method named **openStream**. In our **Handler** class, you create new functionality for this method. In fact, failure to implement this method would result in the Java runtime system throwing an exception, because if this method isn't implemented, the class remains abstract. (Abstract classes cannot be instantiated.)

The **openStream** method opens a data input stream to an object referenced by a URL. It returns an opened input data stream. If the value of the returned data stream is null, the protocol found no viable data. This method takes the URL of an existing Java class as input and returns a suitable input stream for reading the data referenced by the URL. In this method, a piped output stream must be connected to a piped input stream. At one end of the pipe, a thread of a **PipedInputStream** object reads data. At the other end, a thread of a **PipedOutputStream** object writes data.

In the body of the class, enter this code:

```
// Declare the openStream method
public synchronized InputStream openStream(URL u) {
    ... body of method...
}
```

In the next sub-steps of step 6, enter the code in the body of the **openStream** method declared above.

Step 6A: Declare Local Variables In this step, you declare local variables for the **openStream** method. **u.file** is an instance variable of the URL class of the **net.www.html** package and is the file name of the referenced object. **args** is a string containing any command line options entered by the user. **slashindex** is the index of the last slash character in a URL string. Enter these variables in the body of the **openStream** method:

```
String classname = u.file; // class name entered by user
String args; // command line options
int slashindex; // index of slash in URL string
```

Step 6B: Create Data Streams   In this step, you create the required data streams. **poutstream** is an output stream that is connected to an input stream later in the method. **inputstream** is an input stream that is connected to an **outputstream** later in the method. **outputstream** is a print data stream for an output stream. This makes it easier to write to a **PipedOutputStream**. Enter the following code after the local variable statements of the **openStream** method:

```
PipedOutputStream poutstream = new PipedOutputStream();
PipedInputStream inputstream = new PipedInputStream(poutstream);
PrintStream outputstream = new PrintStream(poutstream);
```

Step 6C: Find the Index of the Last Slash of a URL   In this step, you enter code that will find the index of the last slash character in a URL. **classname.lastIndexOf** is a public method of the **String** class of the **java.lang** package. It searches a string backwards to find the last occurrence of a slash character, and returns an integer value. Enter this code fragment after the data stream statements in the **openStream** method:

```
slashindex = classname.lastIndexOf("/");
```

Step 6D: Get the Class Name from the URL   In this step, you enter code that gets the Java class name from the user-supplied URL. This URL is entered in the Document URL window of the HotJava browser. **classname.substring** is a public method of the **String** class in the **java.lang** package. It takes one integer argument, which indicates the starting position in the string of the new substring. This substring is defined from the start index to the end of the string.

```
classname = classname.substring(slashindex + 1);
```

Step 6E: Get Class-Specific Arguments In this step, you enter code that gets any arguments for the referenced class. A user can specify any execution arguments for the class by appending a question mark after the class name in the URL string followed by a colon-separated list of arguments. For example, if the referenced class requires two arguments, they can be specified as part of the URL, such as run:fooClass?goo:roo. The following code changes the class name specification to "fooClass?goo roo", which is then handed to the Java run-time system.

```
// Get class arguments
if (classname.indexOf("?") > 0) {
    classname.replace(':', ' ');
}
```

Step 6F: Force the Type of the User-Specified URL to HTML In this step, you enter code that forces the user-supplied URL to an HTML type document. **u.setType** is a public method of the URL class of the **net.www.html** package. It sets the type of object referenced by a URL. **URL.context_html** is a static public class variable of the same class. Its MIME equivalent is text/html.

```
// Force the URL to HTML type
u.setType(URL.content_html);
```

Step 6G: Write an HTML Document onto a Data Stream In this step, you enter code that writes an HTML document onto an opened **PipedOutputStream**. **outputstream.println** is a public method of the **PipedOutputStream** class of the **java.io** package. Enter this code in the body of the **openStream** method:

```
// Print the new HTML document to the PipedOutputStream
outputstream.
  println("<!DOCTYPE HTML PUBLIC \"-//IETF//DTD HTML 2.0//EN\">");
outputstream.println("<HTML>");
outputstream.print("<TITLE> Running Class: ");
outputstream.print(classname);
outputstream.println(" </TITLE>");
outputstream.print("<BODY><APP CLASS=\"");
outputstream.print(classname);
outputstream.println("\"></BODY>\n</HTML>\n");
```

182

***Step 6H: Close the* PipedOutputStream *and Return the
Input Data Stream*** In this step, you enter code that closes an
open **PipedOutputStream** and returns the opened
PipedInputStream that contains the new HTML document. This is
necessary so that the **PipedInputStream** can be read by the calling
application, which in our example is HotJava. **outputstream.close** is a
public method of the **PipedOutputStream** class of the **java.io** package. Enter this code at the end of the **openStream** method:

```
// Close the ouput stream
outputstream.close();

// Return the PipedInputStream to the HotJava browser
return inputstream;
```

At the end of this chapter, you'll find the complete Java source code
for the **Handler** class presented in part here.

Step 7: Compile the Handler Class

In this step, you compile the Java source code file Handler.java in the
/html/classes/net/www/protocol/run directory. On the command line
enter:

```
javac Handler.java.
```

A successful compile creates a file named Handler.class in the same
directory as the source file.

Step 8: Modify the CLASSPATH Environment Variable

In this step, you include the path to your new protocol handler in the
CLASSPATH environment variable so HotJava can find your new protocol handler. To do this, on the command line enter:

```
setenv CLASSPATH .:/html/classes/:/html/classes/net/www/protocol/run
```

This puts three class repositories into the class path.

1. The dot is the current directory from which HotJava was
   invoked.
2. /html/classes is the path to the HelloWorld class.
3. /html/classes/net/www/protocol/run is the path to the Handler
   class.

(As an alternative, you can alter the CLASSPATH environment variable
in your .cshrc or .profile file.)

Step 9: Test the New run Protocol Handler

In this step, you test your new run protocol handler by running it on the HelloWorld applet class you created in Chapters 1 and 5. Begin by restarting the HotJava browser. If you already have HotJava running, exit and restart it from the shell in which you set the new value for the CLASSPATH variable. If you launch HotJava from some other shell, the CLASSPATH value will be incorrect and the handler won't be available to HotJava.

Then, in the Document URL window of the HotJava browser, enter this URL:

```
run:HelloWorld
```

This renders the string "Hello World!" into the HotJava display window. Figure 9-1 shows what this looks like.

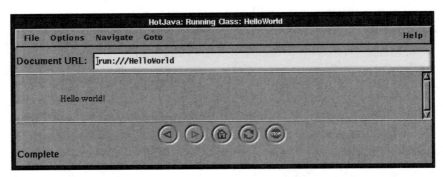

Figure 9-1: Result of the run protocol handler on the HelloWorld applet class.

Content Handler

Just as Java can handle atypical Internet protocols, the HotJava browser can render atypical Web data with a content handler. The purpose of such a handler is to interpret a new or otherwise undefined Multipurpose Internet Mail Extensions (MIME) content type.

MIME is a formal specification for extending the capabilities and functionality of standard e-mail over the Internet. MIME allows you to specify the general type and subtype of data in the body of an e-mail message.

For example, the content handler you write in this section handles the MIME content type called text/plain. The general type is text and the subtype is plain. By comparison, the MIME content type for an

HTML document is text/html. Therefore, the content handler you are about to write helps the HotJava browser to handle plain ASCII text files with a .txt extension.

Steps in Writing the plain text content Handler

In this section, we guide you through the steps required to write and test a plain text content handler. This will be referenced below as plain.

Plain takes responsibility for handling certain files, identified by their file extensions, for the HotJava browser. These files contain pure ASCII text rather than HTML tags and content.

Step 1: Create Directory Structure

In this section, you create four new directories. For this example, assume the /html/classes directory contains your class repository. This is separate from the customary system class library directory structure.

HotJava requires that the directory structure start with a classes directory. The subsequent child directories of **classes—net**, **www**, and **content**—must appear as named and must be created as shown in the following steps. The last directory, **text**, must be named the same as the MIME type of the data.

1. Create a net directory by entering the following on the command line:

```
mkdir /html/classes/net.
```

2. Create a WWW directory by entering the following on the command line:

```
mkdir /html/classes/net/www.
```

3. Create a content directory by entering the following on the command line:

```
mkdir /html/classes/net/www/content.
```

4. Create a text directory by entering the following on the command line:

```
mkdir/html/classes/net/www/content/text.
```

This is the same directory as that of the general MIME type of the data.

Step 2: Create a File Named plain.java

In this step, you create a Java source code file named plain.java with your text editor. This file *must* be in the

185

/html/classes/net/www/content/text directory. Therefore, the absolute path to the content handler source file is: /html/classes/net/www/content/text/plain.java.

The name of the Java source code file should be the MIME subtype of the data. In our example, this is plain. If there were a MIME subtype named bowtie of general type text, you'd expect to find a Java source file named bowtie.java in the same directory.

Step 3: Declare the net.www.content.text Package

In this step, you declare a package named **net.www.content.text** that contains one class named plain. Notice that this corresponds to the MIME subtype of the data in our example. Enter this code at the top of the plain.java source file:

```
// Declare a new package to handle plain text content
package net.www.content.text;
```

Step 4: Import Required System Classes

In this step, you import the required system classes of the class library that are utilized by the plain content handler. Enter these **import** statements after the package declaration:

```
// Methods of this class handle HTML document MIME content
import net.www.html.ContentHandler;
// Methods of this class manipulate URLs
import net.www.html.URL;
// Methods of this class work with data input streams
import java.io.InputStream;
// Methods of this class work with .GIF images
import awt.GifImage;
```

Step 5: Declare the plain Class

In this step, you declare the **plain** class. This class is an extension of the system class named **ContentHandler**. After the **import** statements, enter this code:

```
public class plain extends ContentHandler {
   ... body of class ...
}
```

This declares a public class named **plain** as a subclass or extension of the system class **ContentHandler**. This superclass is part of the

net.www.html system package. It defines an application programming interface for reading the content of objects with arbitrary MIME content types. If you want to declare a new MIME type, you must create a new subclass of **ContentHandler** to decode and render objects of that MIME content type.

Step 6: Declare and Implement the getContent Method

In this step, you declare and write the code for a method named **getContent**. This method gets the content of an object referenced by the URL and is a new implementation of the **getContent** method of the superclass **ContentHandler**. It takes a data input stream starting at the beginning of the referenced object and reads the stream. It appends a string to the object and returns the new object to the browser to render. It takes two arguments, the named input stream and the URL referencing the plain ASCII text file.

Inside the body of the plain class, enter this code:

```
public Object getContent(InputStream is, URL u) {
    ... body of method ...
}
```

In the next sub-steps of step 6, enter the code in the body of the **getContent** method declared above.

Step 6A: Declare Local Variables In this step, you enter local variables for the **getContent** method of the **plain** class. **StringBuffer** is a class of the **java.io** package. Enter this code in the body of the **getContent** method:

```
StringBuffer sb = new StringBuffer(); // buffer of ASCII data
int c; // individual character of input stream
```

Step 6B: Read the Input Stream In this step, you enter code that reads the input stream one character at a time. It also appends a string to a buffer. **is.read** is a public method of the **InputStream** class of the **java.io** package. **sb.appendChar** is a public method of the **StringBuffer** class that appends a character to a string. **sb.append** is a public method of the **StringBuffer** class that appends a string to another string. This method appends the string "This is a plain ASCII text file." to the current input data stream that contains an ASCII text file. Enter this code:

```
// Read the input stream and append a character
while ((c = is.read()) >= 0) {
    sb.appendChar((char)c); // fill buffer with each character
}


// Append a string to another
sb.append("\n\nThis is a plain ASCII text file.\n");
```

Step 6C: Close the Input Stream and Return the New String

In this step, you enter code that closes the data input stream and returns the new **Object** to the HotJava browser. **sb.toString** is a public method of the **StringBuffer** class and converts a string buffer to a string. **is.close** is a public method of the **InputStream** class. It closes an open input data stream. Enter this code at the end of the **getContent** method:

```
// Close the input data stream
is.close();


// Return the new string object to HotJava
return sb.toString();
```

Step 7: Compile the plain Class

In this step, you compile the Java source code file plain.java in the /html/classes/net/www/content/text directory. On the command line, enter:

```
javac plain.java
```

A successful compile creates a class file named plain.class in the same directory as the source file.

Step 8: Create an ASCII Text File Named test.txt

In this step, you create an ASCII file named test.txt in the root directory. So, the absolute file name is /test.txt. With your text editor, enter this ASCII text in a file and save it as test.txt:

```
All generalizations are false, even this one!
```

```
All it takes is lightnin' fast reflexes and a considerable amount of
snake-eyed concentration.
```

Step 9: Modify the CLASSPATH Environment Variable

For HotJava to find your new content handler, you must include the path to the Java class file named plain.class. To do this, on the command line enter:

188

```
setenv CLASSPATH.:/html/classes/:/html/classes/net/www/content/text
```

This puts three class repositories into the class path.

1. The dot is the current directory from which HotJava is invoked.
2. /html/classes is the path to the HelloWorld class.
3. /html/classes/net/www/content/text is the path to the plain class.

As an alternative, you can alter the CLASSPATH environment variable in your .cshrc or .profile file.

Step 10: Remove the text/plain mailcap Entry

In this step, you comment out any handlers that have been predefined for the text/plain entry in your .mailcap file to test the handler you've just written. Here's how to do it on a UNIX system: Look for a file named .mailcap in your home user directory and edit it with a text editor. Find the line that contains an entry including the string "text/plain" and insert a pound sign ("#") at the beginning of that line.

For non-UNIX platforms, you typically have to check for Java-capable browser-related configuration files. After you find the file that specifies MIME types, simply comment out or remove the text/plain entry.

Step 11: Test the New plain Content Handler

In this step, you test your new plain content handler. You instruct the HotJava browser to render the test.txt file plus the appended string "This is a plain ASCII text file." specified in the plain class source code.

Begin by restarting your HotJava browser. If you have HotJava already running, exit and restart it from the shell in which you set the new value of the CLASSPATH variable. If you launch HotJava from some other shell, the CLASSPATH value will be incorrect and the handler won't be available to HotJava.

Next, enter this URL in the Document URL window of the HotJava browser: file:/test.txt.

This renders the new object—the ASCII text file plus the appended string—into the HotJava display window. Figure 9-2 shows what this looks like.

Class Sources

This section provides the complete listing of both handlers described in this chapter.

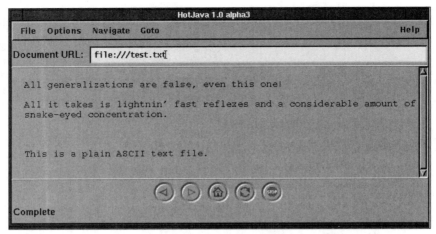

Figure 9-2: Result of the plain text content handler on an ASCII file

Handler Class

```
// Declare that the following class is part of this package
package net.www.protocol.run

// Include classes to handle input and output
import java.io.*;
// Include classes to handle HTML document content
import net.www.html.*;

// Declare the new run Handler class
class Handler extends URLStreamHandler {

    public synchronized InputStream openStream(URL u) {

        // Declare local variables.
        String classname = u.file; // class name entered by user
        String args; // command line options
        int slashindex; // index of slash in URL string

        // Create data streams
        PipedOutputStream poutstream = new PipedOutputStream();
        PipedInputStream inputstream = new PipedInputStream(poutstream);
        PrintStream outputstream = new PrintStream(poutstream);

        // Get index of last "/" in URL
        slashindex = classname.lastIndexOf("/");
```

190

```
    // Get class name from URL
    classname = classname.substring(slashindex + 1);

    //Get any arguments for the referenced class
    if (classname.indexOf("?") > 0) {
      classname.replace(':', ' ');
    }

    // Force the URL to HTML type
    u.setType(URL.content_html);

    // Print the new HTML document to the PipedOutputStream
    outputstream.println
      ("<!DOCTYPE HTML PUBLIC \"-//IETF//DTD HTML 2.0//EN\">");
    outputstream.println("<HTML>");
    outputstream.print("<TITLE> Running Class: ");
    outputstream.print(classname);
    outputstream.println(" </TITLE>");
    outputstream.print("<BODY><APP CLASS=\"");
    outputstream.print(classname);
    outputstream.println("\"></BODY>\n</HTML>\n");

    // Close the PipedOutputStream
    outputstream.close();

    // Return the PipedInputStream to the HotJava browser
    return inputstream;
  }
}
```

plain Class

```
// Declare a new package to handle plain text content
package net.www.content.text;

// Methods of this class handle HTML document MIME content
import net.www.html.ContentHandler;
// Methods of this class manipulate URLs
import net.www.html.URL;
// Methods of this class work with data input streams
import java.io.InputStream;
// Methods of this class work with .GIF images
```

```
import awt.GifImage;

public class plain extends ContentHandler {

    // Gets the content of an object referenced by the URL
    public Object getContent(InputStream is, URL u) {

        // Declare local variables
        StringBuffer sb = new StringBuffer();// buffer of ASCII data
        int c; // individual character of input stream

        // Read the input stream one character at a time
        while ((c = is.read()) >= 0) {
            sb.appendChar((char)c); // fill buffer with each character
        }

        // Append the string to the current string buffer
        sb.append("\n\nThis is a plain ASCII text file.\n");

        // Close the data input stream
        is.close();

        // Return the new Object to the HotJava browser
        return sb.toString();
    }
}
```

Summary

With Java, you can extend the HotJava browser in two ways: to handle new protocols and to handle new data types. This permits an unprecedented degree of extensibility and flexibility to the Java environment, especially at run time, when handlers for protocols and content can be loaded on the fly.

This exercise of working with handlers ends our hands-on coverage of the Java language. In the next and final chapter, we put on our prognostication hats to assess the current state of Java and speculate about its future. We think this offers an exciting conclusion to our discussion of this unique and powerful programming language.

## CHAPTER 10

The Future of Java

What about Today?

With only a 1.0 version of its specification and only alpha release code currently available, Java is still in its infancy. Today, we'd have to say that, while Java certainly offers interesting capabilities, its most useful applications still remain slightly over the horizon.

As this future is realized, what we call Java today may very well be called something else. Nevertheless, it's clear from the enthusiastic reception that Java has received on the Web that a powerful demand exists for client-side interactivity and data manipulation (i.e., applets), just as ample demand exists for a network- and Internet-aware, cross-platform application development environment like that supplied by the Java compiler, its interpreter, and its runtime system.

As we close this investigation of Java, the real questions we'd like to tackle are:

- What is Java good for today?
- What are Java's most serious limitations?

These are the topics for the two sections that follow.

What's Java Good for Today?

The short and sweet answer to this question is, "Lots!" In perusing Sun's home page for Java and HotJava, with its numerous offshoots and ties to interested third parties, we found much finished code to consider. In fact, as of late summer, 1995, more than 100 applets and more than a couple of dozen full-blown Java applications were available. To see the most current listings, check out Sun's Cool Applets page at http://java.sun.com/applets/. This URL also includes pointers to third-party examples.

Enough examples of what's available in this realm exist that Sun broke its listings into numerous categories. Here's a list of those categories, plus annotations about some of the more interesting examples we uncovered:

Tools to spice up HTML documents:

* New and improved "nervous text"

http://www.spd.eee.strath.ac.uk/~matthew/java/NervousText.html

* A general-purpose animation applet

http://java.sun.com/applets/applets/animator/index.html

* An animated "under construction" graphic with sound

http://java.sun.com/applets/applets/construction/index.html

* Dynamically-generated color bullets

http://java.sun.com/applets/applets/bullets/index.html

Educational applets:

* View 3-D chemical models

http://java.sun.com/applets/applets/ChemicalModels/index.html

* Fractal figure display code

http://java.sun.com/applets/applets/fractal/index.html

* Statistics: animated sampling distributions

http://www.thomtech.com/~suresh/java

* Sort Applets: demos of various sort algorithms

http://www.cs.ubc.ca/spider/harrison/Java/sorting-demo.html

Utilities:

- WebTap: stress tester for web servers

`http://www.ebt.com/WebTap/home.html`

- HTML sizer applet: displays total size of an HTML page, including images and applets

`http://www.starwave.com/people/jpayne/sizer.html`

- Search applets: automated access to Lycos and Yahoo

`http://java.sun.com/applets/applets/websearch/index.html`

- Bar chart applet: control over text, color, orientation

`http://java.sun.com/applets/applets/barchart/index.html`

Programming Tips:

- Jarchive: a class to store multiple byte arrays, similar to a tar file; includes example of modified Animator class that uses Jarchives so that it needs to load only one Jarchive, instead of multiple .GIF files, improving applet load time

`http://www.cs.brown.edu/people/amd/java/jar/`

- ActiveButton and ActiveLink: applets that act like GUI buttons; can be configured with normal, active, and pushed images, or animation sequences. ActiveLink is an example subclass of ActiveButton that acts like a hyperlink

`http://www-dse.doc.ic.ac.uk/~np2/java/button/button.html`

- HotJava performance tests and test harness

`http://java.sun.com/applets/applets/performance/index.html`

- Enhanced user interfaces through embedded applets

`http://www.starwave.com/people/jpayne/java/`

Snazzy Demos:

- A spinning globe powered by Java

`http://www.process.com/Launch/launchpd.htm`

- Sun's financial portfolio graphing demo

`http://java.sun.com/applets/applets/stockdemo/standalone.html`

In addition, there's plenty of work underway at Sun and other places to build interactive, distributed applications using Java. We found

numerous pointers to information on applications such as HTML validation tools, HTML document management, parsing tools, and applet execution environments.

What Are Java's Limitations?

Currently, the biggest beefs from the development community regarding Java fall squarely into three areas. These are:

- **Documentation**

  In an August 1995 article in *WebWeek*, an anonymous programmer
  says: "The biggest problem that I see [with HotJava] is that the documentation is truly abysmal." This sentiment is widely shared in
  the community, and extends to more than HotJava, if our experience is any indication. But it's not atypical of a new development
  area, in which code often gets ahead of its documentation.
  Perhaps this will change by the time you read this book.

- **Lack of broad platform support**

  It's widely believed that the only reasonable development environments for Java today are Windows NT and Solaris 2.X, and require
  high-end machines like SparcStations and Pentium PCs (90 MHz or
  better). Despite discussions about Windows 95, MacOS 7.5, and other
  flavors of UNIX, the technology's not yet available to the masses.

- **Concerns about performance**

  Although Java's architecture is platform independent, its runtime
  system is perceived by many developers as somewhat slow and
  not in the same league as compiled C. Most observers expect
  Sun's delivery of its inline native compiler will overcome current
  performance concerns, perhaps by the time you read this.

We agree with all of these assessments. But we are cautiously opti-
mistic, especially in view of Java's reception from the development
community—even as an alpha release. Java obviously promises to fill
lots of needs that are currently unmet in other Web- and Internet-
focused application environments. This is why, as you'll see in the next
section, we expect great things from Java in the future.

What Kinds of Applications Should You Expect in the Future?

While we're not 100% sure that all of these applications will be coded
in Java, we're pretty sure that they'll partake of much of its approach

and capabilities, albeit with significant extensions. Nevertheless, we expect Java and related development efforts to spawn a whole new class of interactive applications right away and into the foreseeable future. And, we expect it to be pretty exciting stuff—not just for entertainment, but for all kinds of practical uses too.

Current research is aimed at remedying the most obvious deficiencies in Java's current implementation. Significant efforts are already underway to:

- beef up the user interface with better tools and widgets;
- expand current foundation classes and class libraries with a broader and more useful set of tools;
- improve performance, system documentation, and developer support; and
- broaden the base of suitable development platforms.

The question we raised at the beginning of this chapter is hard to answer specifically (as we don't have a crystal ball—virtual or otherwise), so prior to hazarding educated guesses at some answers, we'd like to restate it as: "What kind of applications will Java make possible?"

We certainly expect to see more powerful capabilities for users to interact with large collections of data. Right now, a request for WAIS access through Java tops Sun's list of requested Java enhancements. This points to the strong perceived need for users to formulate queries and process results at their own workstations. Likewise, the ability to search, sort, and report the results of such queries is important, as applets for statistical analysis, graphing, charting, and sorting already indicate.

In a similar vein, we expect to see the delivery of complete text search engines at the user level. Today, one limitation that's hampering widespread use of HTML as a format for static documents, like those published on CD-ROMs, is the lack of a client-side search engine to help users query and interact with local data quickly and effectively. A full-blown Java search engine would let any user with access to a Web browser and a Java runtime system read the same CD-ROM, irrespective of platform.

At a far finer level of detail, Java applets could help to organize data received on the fly and let users interact with it immediately. Once data collections are downloaded to the user's workstation, they could also be manipulated locally, without having to wait on background processing of server requests. This could not only improve the kinds and quality of interaction, it would help to speed such things up! For example, analyses of a subset of a product information database could be performed on a local version—downloaded once at the beginning of a session and manipulated locally thereafter with only occasional checks to make sure the data are still fresh.

In short, we expect this kind of technology to have a sweeping impact on the way we view and use the Web, from the basic interactive behavior of what are now static documents to the ability to localize and interact with on-line databases, either in whole or in part. Likewise, we also believe that Java-enabled Web browsers can deliver cross-platform access to large collections of textual, graphical, and other kinds of information that today require platform-specific hypertext and search engines.

What Barriers Remain?

Given that we can conceive of these capabilities today, what prevents their immediate realization? In large part, we still lack support for the full range of consumer platforms in use. We expect this to be remedied by the middle of 1996. It will probably take longer for the full gamut of Web browsers to adopt Java technology; and without broad demand for its support, Java won't become ubiquitous soon.

What's sorely needed is a set of standards for the kinds of extensions to Java that we've discussed here. It's widely recognized that supporting interactivity and client-side capability on the Web will require this functionality to be present in the majority of browsers. And while Netscape Communications has announced their intention to license Java for use in their wildly popular Netscape Navigator (itself available on several flavors of UNIX; on Windows NT, 95, and 3.x; on the Macintosh; and on other platforms), it's not clear what they'll use Java for, or what level of commitment this could elicit from other browser vendors.

Likewise, there's still a strong need for the kind of widespread support from the development community for Java that CGI programming has generated. Today, literally thousands of CGI libraries, tools, and applications are available for downloading. Also available is a large body of collective expertise in using these tools and technologies to enhance the quality of information delivered on the Web, and to improve the Web's extensibility and its customization to individual users' needs and preferences. It's clear that Java is promising in its ability to further improve these areas; it's just not clear that the kind of universal adoption and enthusiasm that's needed to make Java part and parcel of the Web has arrived yet, or that it's imminent.

In fact, outside Sun Microsystems, Java-based development efforts are currently fragmentary and disjointed. Also, these efforts aren't now directly aimed at standardization. Until initial research and more sample implementations are completed and an agreed-upon set of classes, methods, and constructors has been developed for Java, standardization would be premature. Ultimately, Sun may have to let go of Java and bequeath it to a consortium or to the public domain—much as Novell did with the UNIX trademark and that operating system's source code if the language is to truly succeed and attain universality.

Yet, widespread use of interactive Web technology won't be possible until meaningful standards can be defined and deployed. That's the inevitable paradox involved in adopting and adapting to new technologies like Java: It's necessary to push development as far and as fast as possible, but the results of such labors can only become widespread when they've settled down enough to be somewhat stable and standardized.

Given the demands of constructing a complete lexicon of objects, classes, methods, and constructors for a fully-realized interactive Web, it's also safe to say that some platform limitations still are holding back its delivery to the average desktop computer. While Moore's Law makes it clear that ever-more-capable computers are just around the corner, these demands still won't be met for awhile.

Despite these limitations, we can't help but see Java as a meaningful step toward the widespread delivery of a usefully interactive World Wide Web environment to the average Internet user. Yet, Java appears to have evoked a strong response in both development and user communities, and has certainly raised the level of activity and interest surrounding the topic of cross-platform, client-side Web capabilities.

In fact, we believe that technology and interface ergonomics, coupled with decreasing costs and increasing capabilities for computing, make the movement toward a fully-interactive Web both inevitable and inexorable. A huge mass of problems, details, and implementation issues may stand in the way right now, but they probably won't be allowed to stay there for long!

Summary

Throughout this book, we've explored Java's current structures and capabilities, while trying to understand its motivation and technical limitations. In this chapter, we've extended our scope to speculate on what Java could mean to the future of networking and computing in general. We've extended its potential impact from widgets in HTML documents to tools capable of searching, organizing, and managing large collections of data. We hope we haven't lost your enthusiasm or understanding along the way.

In closing, we'd like to leave you with an annotated list of Web sites that you can use to extend your own studies of Java and related phenomena and technologies. We sincerely hope that you've found our coverage useful and illuminating, and that you'll continue investigations on your own. In an area as new and fluid as Web-based interactivity, there's no substitute for staying current with emerging theories, technologies, and implementations. Our concluding list of Web resources should help you keep track of the companies, technologies, and people that are making Java happen.

Noteworthy Java Resources

- Sun's Java Home page

```
http://java.sun.com/index.html
```

- Java FAQ, version 2

```
http://java.sun.com/faq2.html
```

- HotJava user's guide

```
http://java.sun.com/1.0alpha3/doc/misc/using.html
```

- The HotJava Security story (great bibliography)

```
http://java.sun.com/1.0alpha3/doc/security/security.html
```

- List of frequently-requested features for Java

```
http://java.sun.com/FrequentlyRequestedFeatures.html
```

- List of known Java bugs and problems

```
http://java.sun.com/KnownBugs.html
```

- Tutorial on writing and using Java applets

http://java.sun.com/1.0alpha3/doc/appguide/index.html

- Java- and HotJava-related mailing lists

http://java.sun.com/mail.html

- Java and HotJava HyperMail mailing list archives

http://java.sun.com/archives/index.html

- Links to most of Sun's on-line Java and HotJava documentation

http://java.sun.com/documentation.html

- The Design of Distributed Hyperlinked Programming Documentation (IWHD '95; a paper about Java's Web-based API documentation, written by Lisa Friendly, a Java team technical writer)

http://java.sun.com/people/friendly/iwhd.ps

- Overview of the HotJava browser

http://java.sun.com/1.0alpha3/doc/overview/hotjava/index.html

- Java language overview

http://java.sun.com/1.0alpha3/doc/overview/java/index.html

- Java language environment and its operation (white paper)

http://java.sun.com/whitePaper/javawhitepaper_1.html

We hope we've given you the information you need to get familiar with Java, or maybe even to start some Java applet or application construction on your own. Whatever your objectives, we hope you achieve them!

The Java
System API

*t*he Java and HotJava system provides an application programming interface. This API allows programmers to create Java
programs that can interact with a well-developed library of
predefined classes.

For example, to manipulate text strings in a C program you might
rely on built-in, language-specific string functions such as **strlen,
strcpy**, and **strcmp**. In Java, these were deliberately omitted as function calls to make the language compact and simple. Instead, Java's
implementers provide a collection of classes that supply not only
string-handling capabilities, but also a variety of other functions that
extend the functionality of the Java language without burdening it with
a large number of intrinsic capabilities. Only those classes that are actually referenced are linked into a Java executable, which helps to manage
the size and complexity of your applications. This can be critical for
client operating systems such as Microsoft Windows, in which size and
complexity can make the difference between usability and uselessness.

The Java system class library is organized as a collection of packages for the Java language and the HotJava browser. Each package contains an interface and a collection of classes. For each interface and class, we present the related class variables, constructors, methods, and exceptions. In this appendix, you learn about the packages and classes in the Java system library, and how to use them.

Java Packages

Here, we cover the packages available in the system class library. These packages are relevant to the Java programming language, to its utility classes and methods, and to its input/output-related classes and methods.

java.lang

The **java.lang** package contains Java language classes and interfaces. These entities implement language details such as data types (e.g., Boolean, character, string), execution threads, and system calls. You import all the classes and interfaces in the **java.lang** package by including the following statement in your source code:

```
import java.lang.*; /* include all objects in the java.lang package */
```

Table A-1 provides a summary of the **java.lang** package that includes its interface, and all of its classes and exceptions.

Table A-1: Interface, Classes, and Exceptions of the java.lang Package

PACKAGE ELEMENT	NAME	DESCRIPTION
Interface	Runnable	provides a common protocol for objects that need to execute code while the objects are active
Class	Boolean	a wrapper for Boolean objects
	Character	a wrapper for character objects
	Class	contains runtime representations of system and user-defined classes
	ClassLoader*	defines policies for loading Java classes in the runtime system
	Double	wrapper for double-precision values

Table A-1: *Continued*

PACKAGE ELEMENT	NAME	DESCRIPTION
	Float	wrapper for single-precision values
	Integer	wrapper for 32-bit integer values
	Long	wrapper for 64-bit integer values
	Math	math library
	Number*	superclass of numeric scalars—integer, long, float, and double
	Object	root of system class hierarchy; parent of all objects
	Ref	used by Java's garbage collector
	String	wrapper for constant text strings
	StringBuffer	dynamic buffer for characters and strings
	System	provides access to system functions
	Thread	provides support for multithreaded execution
	ThreadDeath	used for explicit cleanup after asynchronous termination
Exception	AbstractMethod Exception	signals attempt to call an abstract method
	Arithmetic Exception	signals arithmetic error
	ArrayIndexOutOf BoundsException	signals invalid array index
	ClassCast Exception	signals invalid cast of class
	DataFormat Exception	signals invalid data format
	Exception	parent class of all exceptions
	FileFormat Exception	signals invalid file format

Table A-1: *Continued*

PACKAGE ELEMENT	NAME	DESCRIPTION
	FileNotFound Exception	signals file not found
	IOException	signals input and output error
	IllegalAccess Exception	signals illegal object access
	IllegalArgument Exception	signals invalid argument
	IllegalState Exception	signals illegal object state
	IncompatibleClass ChangeException	signals illegal class change
	IncompatibleType Exception	signals incompatible class change
	InternalException	signals internal system error
	NegativeArraySize Exception	signals negative array length
	NoClassDefFound Exception	signals class definition not found
	NoSuchElement Exception	signals an empty enumeration
	NoSuchMethod Exception	signals a method not found
	NullPointer Exception	signals use of null pointer
	NumberFormat Exception	signals bad numeric format
	OutOfMemory Exception	signals insufficient system memory
	StackOverflow Exception	signals execution stack overflow
	StringIndexOutOf RangeException	signals index of string out of range

Table A-1: *Continued*

PACKAGE ELEMENT	NAME	DESCRIPTION
	UnloadableClass Exception	signals class can't be loaded
	UnsatisfiedLink Exception	signals link not completed

* abstract class

java.util

The **java.util** package contains a single interface, along with a list of classes and exceptions related to utility operations in the Java programming environment. To include all the interfaces, classes, and exceptions in this package, use this Java statement:

```
import java.util.*; /* import all items of java.util package */
```

Table A-2 provides a summary of the interface, the classes, and the exception in the **java.util** package.

Table A-2: Interface, Classes, and Exception of the java.util Package

PACKAGE ELEMENT	NAME	DESCRIPTION
Interface	Enumeration	specifies a set of methods used to enumerate a set of values
Class	ConditionLock	provides a mechanism to wait for the setting of a state variable followed by the acquisition of a lock
	Date	wrapper for the system date
	HashTable	maps keys to values
	Linker	allows the system to dynamically link new native method libraries
	Lock	provides mechanism to lock access to system resources
	ObjectScope	methods used by debuggers to look into objects

Table A-2: *Continued*

PACKAGE ELEMENT	NAME	DESCRIPTION
	Stack	methods to manipulate a first-in, first-out stack of objects
	StringTokenizer	methods to linearly tokenize a string
	Vector	methods for manipulating a dynamic array
Exception	EmptyStack Exception	signals that the stack is empty

java.io

The **java.io** package contains interfaces, classes, and exceptions that provide input and output manipulation capabilities for the Java programming environment. To import the interface, the classes, and the exception in this package, use the following import statement:

```
import java.io.*; // imports all items in java.io package
```

Table A-3 is a summary of the interface, the classes, and the exception in the **java.io** package.

Table A-3: Interface, Classes, and Exception of the java.io Package

PACKAGE ELEMENT	NAME	DESCRIPTION
Interface	FilenameFilter	provides interface for system file names
Class	AccessError Handler	provides file access control
	BufferedInput Stream	provides fast reading of stream characters
	BufferedOutput Stream	provides fast writing of stream characters
	DataInputStream	provides portable reading of primitive Java data types
	DataOutputStream	provides portable writing of primitive Java data types

Table A-3: *Continued*

PACKAGE ELEMENT	NAME	DESCRIPTION
	File	provides a wrapper for system files
	FileInputStream	provides input file mechanisms
	FileOutputStream	provides output file mechanisms
	FilterInputStream*	represents filtered input stream of bytes
	FilterOutputStream*	represents filtered output stream of bytes
	InputStream*	represents an input stream of bytes
	InputStreamBuffer	provides access to an input buffer
	InputStream Sequence	provides mechanism to convert a sequence of input streams into an input stream
	InpuStream StringBuffer	implements a String buffer that can be used as an input stream
	OutputStream*	represents output stream of bytes
	OutputStreamBuffer	provides a buffer that can be used as an output stream
	PipedInputStream	provides a piped input stream
	PipedOutputStream	provides a piped output stream
	PrintStream	provides mechanisms for writing an output stream
	PushbackInput Stream	implements an input stream with a one-byte, push-back buffer
	RandomAccessFile	provides mechanisms for manipulating random access files
	StreamTokenizer	provides mechanisms to translate an input stream into a stream of tokens
Exception	SecurityException	signals security exception

* abstract class

HotJava Packages

In this section, you learn about the packages in the system class library that provide an API to the HotJava browser. These packages implement windowing activities, network functions, and browser capabilities. You can use them to write extensions to the HotJava browser itself, or you can use them in your own applets.

awt

The **awt** package implements most of HotJava's common windowing activities and functionality. It defines numerous interfaces, many classes, and a plethora of exceptions. To include all of the interfaces and classes of this package, use this code:

```
import awt.*; // import all items in awt package
```

Table A-4 summarizes the items defined in the **awt** package.

Table A-4: The Interfaces and Classes of the awt Package

PACKAGE ELEMENT	NAME	DESCRIPTION
Interface	ChoiceHandler	maps callbacks of window functions
	Dialog boxes	contains common elements of dialog
	DialogHandler	defines three callbacks (OK, cancel, and help) of MessageDialog class
	EventHandler	defines interface for objects that must handle events
	Layoutable	provides mechanism for layout of windows and DisplayItems
	Scrollable	interface for objects providing vertical and horizontal scrolling
	Scrollbarable	interface for objects controlled by a scrollbar
Class	BorderLayout	provides control of window border layout
	Button	provides a native GUI button

Table A-4: *Continued*

PACKAGE ELEMENT	NAME	DESCRIPTION
	ChildList	provides hierarchical mechanisms that map names to Layoutable objects
	Color	provides wrapper for RGB colors
	Column	wrapper of column object
	ColumnLayout	provides mechanisms for control of column layout
	Component	parent class of all native GUI elements
	Container	provides mechanisms for wrapping other windows and frames
	ContainerLayout*	represents container layout for various containers
	DIBitmap	provides mechanisms to manipulate device-independent, 8-bit images and their color maps
	DIWUpdateRequest	provides mechanisms to manipulate device-independent windows
	Dimension	provides a wrapper for objects that possess height and width
	DisplayItem	provides mechanism to embed objects inside a DisplayItemWindow
	DisplayItemWindow	provides mechanisms to embed a DisplayItem in a window
	Event	implements a platform-independent wrapper to handle events from native GUI items
	EventRepeater	implements a thread that repeatedly invokes an event handler
	FileDialog	implements a native GUI file dialog box
	FlowLayout	provides control of layout flow of GUI buttons in a panel

Table A-4: *Continued*

Package Element	Name	Description
	FocusManager	provides management of window focus
	Font	provides creation of new fonts
	FontMetrics	provides font metric mechanisms
	FontSpec	provides a wrapper of font properties
	FontTable	provides mechanisms to create native fonts
	Formatter	provides control for layout of a set of DisplayItems in a window
	Formatting Parameters	provides a wrapper for Formatter state variables
	Frame	implements a top-level window container for other windows
	GapsLayout*	represents object layout containing spans of white space
	GenericGraphics	defines base class for all graphics contexts for devices
	GifImage	provides .GIF image conversion mechanisms
	Graphics	provides a wrapper for graphics context of a window
	Image*	represents an image
	ImageDisplayItem	provides a DisplayItem for an embedded image
	Label	displays read-only text
	List	implements a scrollable list of textual items
	Menu	implements an element of a MenuBar
	MenuBar	provides a wrapper for a native MenuBar tied to a frame

Table A-4: *Continued*

PACKAGE ELEMENT	NAME	DESCRIPTION
	MenuItem	represents a chosen item from a Menu
	MessageDialog	provides control of a dialog box presented to the user that contains a message
	NativeDisplayItem	creates a wrapper for native GUI component operations to a DisplayItem
	OptionMenu	implements a pop-up menu of choices
	PSGraphics	provides a wrapper for PostScript files
	RadioGroup	provides control mechanisms for mutual-exclusion radio buttons
	Row	implements mechanisms for a row of window elements
	RowColLayout	provides mechanisms to control row and column layout of window components
	RowLayout	provides mechanisms to control layout of a row of window components
	Scrollbar	implements a native GUI scrollbar object
	ScrollbarAction*	represents a scrollbar callback
	SmoothScroller	provides control of window scrolling
	Space	provides white space to a layout
	StringDialog	presents a native dialog box containing a message, a text input area, and OK, cancel, and help buttons
	Text	provides a container for lines of text
	TextArea	provides a container for multiple lines of text that can be edited

Table A-4: *Continued*

PACKAGE ELEMENT	NAME	DESCRIPTION
	TextDisplayItem	provides mechanisms to control properties of displayed text
	TextField	implements a GUI single-line text input widget
	TextWindow	displays formatted text in a window
	Toggle	implements a GUI item with a Boolean state
	WSFontMetrics	implements a FontMetrics object for a WServer font
	WServer	provides direct interaction with the native GUI
	Window	provides a general-purpose container for other windows and window elements
	XbmImage	implements mechanisms to parse X bitmap images
	Xpm2Image	implements mechanisms to parse X pixmap images

* abstract class

browser

The **browser** package contains interfaces and classes that provide an API to the HotJava browser's general functionality and capabilities. To import all the interfaces and classes of this package, use the following import statement:

```
import browser.*; // import all items of browser package
```

Table A-5 summarizes the interfaces and classes of the **browser** package.

Table A-5: The Interfaces and Classes of the browser Package

PACKAGE ELEMENT	NAME	DESCRIPTION
Interface	Alignable	allows alignment of a Displayitem
	Observer	?????????????
Class	AnchorStyle	manipulates an anchor stack associated with a Formatter

Table A-5: *Continued*

PACKAGE ELEMENT	NAME	DESCRIPTION
	AnchorTagRef	represents either a source or a target anchor (i.e., <A>) in an HTML document
	AppTagRef	represents the <APP> HTML tag
	Applet	represents a base applet class
	AppletDisplayItem	provides a placeholder for applets
	BasicStyle	specifies basic style characteristics of HTML tag references
	BreakingStyle	provides paragraph breaks
	DDTagRef	provides rendering mechanisms for <DD> tag
	DLTagRef	provides rendering mechanisms for <DL> tag
	DTTagRef	provides rendering mechanisms for <DT> tag
	DisplayItemTagRef	superclass of all HotJava HTML tag references that result from creation of DisplayItems
	Document	associates specific style changes with particular HTML tags and provides control of applets
	DocumentManager	provides management mechanisms for HTML documents
	DocumentRef	???????????????
	FormTagRef	defines a <FORM> tag object
	HRDisplayItem	provides an <HR> horizontal rule
	HRTagRef	provides rendering mechanisms for <HR> tag
	HistoryVector	provide history tracking mechanisms
	ImageCache	provides mechanisms to manipulate images in cache
	ImageHandle	provides mechanisms to manipulate

215

Table A-5: *Continued*

PACKAGE ELEMENT	NAME	DESCRIPTION
		image handles
	ImageReader	provides a thread of execution that waits for image fetch requests from ImageHandle
	ImgTagRef	provide rendering mechanism for <IMG> HTML tag
	InputTagRef	defines <INPUT> tag mechanisms
	LITagRef	defines <LI> tag mechanisms
	OLTagRef	defines <OL> tag mechanisms
	Observable	provides mechanisms to manage ???????
	ObserverList	???????????????
	OptionTagRef	defines <OPTION> tag mechanisms
	ProgressDialog	defines a dialog box that presents current execution progress messages
	ProgressWindow	provides window canvas for display of execution progress
	Properties	implements a hash table that can be saved and loaded from a stream; describes persistent properties
	SecurityDialog	provides a dialog box displaying security messages
	Style	provides style changes occurring from HTML tag references
	StyleTagRef	provides mechanisms to manipulate HTML tag styles
	ULTagRef	defines <UL> tag mechanism
	URLHistory	provides tracking of URLs visited
	WRFormatter	depreciated WebRunner element
	WRImageItem	depreciated WebRunner element
	WRListRef	depreciated WebRunner element

Table A-5: *Continued*

PACKAGE ELEMENT	NAME	DESCRIPTION
	WRTagRef	depreciated WebRunner element
	WRTextItem	depreciated WebRunner element
	WRWindow	depreciated WebRunner element
	hotjava	provides management of the GUI components of HotJava

Question marks indicate names not currently defined in the Java specification.

browser.audio

The **browser.audio** Java system package contains classes that provide mechanisms to manipulate and play an audio stream. To include all the classes in this package, use the following Java code:

```
// import all items in the browser.audio package
import browser.audio.*;
```

Table A-6 summarizes the classes in the **browser.audio** package.

Table A-6: Classes of the browser.audio Package

PACKAGE ELEMENT	NAME	DESCRIPTION
Class	AudioData*	provides a mechanism to prepare sounds files to play
	AudioDataStream	constructs a stream of audio data to play
	AudioPlayer	provides mechanisms to play multiple channels of audio on one channel
	AudioStream	provides conversion from InputStream to AudioInputStream
	AudioStream Sequence	provides conversion of a sequence of input stream data into a single input stream
	ContinuousAudio DataStream	provides a continuous stream of audio data

* abstract class

net

The **net** package provides general network functions and capabilities. To include all classes and exceptions of this package, use the following Java code:

```
import net.*; // import all items of the net package
```

Table A-7 summarizes the classes and exceptions in the **net** package.

Table A-7: Classes and Exceptions of the net Package

PACKAGE ELEMENT	NAME	DESCRIPTION
Class	Firewall	provides firewall manipulation mechanisms
	InetAddress	provides Internet address information retrieval
	NetworkClient	base class for network clients; provides basic network client mechanisms
	NetworkServer	base class for network servers; provides basic network server functionality
	ProgressData	?????????????
	ProgressEntry	?????????????
	Socket	provides TCP socket manipulation methods
	TelnetInputStream	provides mechanisms to manipulate telnet input data streams
	TelnetOutputStream	provides mechanisms to manipulate telnet output data streams
	TransferProtocol Client	implements a general interface to common file transfer protocols
Exception	ProtocolException	signals network protocol exception EPROTO
	SOCKSException	signals SOCKS error occurred while using a socket

Table A-7: *Continued*

PACKAGE ELEMENT	NAME	DESCRIPTION
	SocketException	signals error while using a socket
	TelnetProtocol Exception	signals client received bogus result from telnet server
	UnknownHost Exception	signals host address requested is not resolvable
	UnknownService Exception	signals requested port is unknown

Question marks indicate names not currently defined in the Java specification.

net.ftp

The **net.ftp** package provides a specialized API for TCP/IP-based file transfer protocol (FTP) functions and capabilities. To import all classes and exceptions in this package, use this Java code:

```
import net.ftp.*; // import all items in net.ftp package
```

Table A-8 summarizes the classes and exceptions for the **net.ftp** package.

Table A-8: Classes and Exceptions of the net.ftp Package

PACKAGE ELEMENT	NAME	DESCRIPTION
Class	FtpClient	implements an FTP client
	FtpInputStream	provides manipulation mechanisms for an FTP input stream
	IftpClient	implements an FTP client that uses a proxy server to pass through a firewall boundary
Exception	FtpLoginException	signals error during FTP login
	FtpProtocol Exception	signals error during FTP session

net.nntp

The **net.nntp** package contains special network news transfer protocol (NNTP) functions and capabilities. To include all classes and exceptions in this package, use this Java code:

```
import net.nntp.*; /* import all items of the net.nntp protocol */
```

Table A-9 summarizes the classes and exceptions in the **net.nntp** package.

Table A-9: Classes and Exceptions of the net.nntp Package

PACKAGE ELEMENT	NAME	DESCRIPTION
Class	NewsgroupInfo	provides management of status information of newsgroups
	NntpClient	implements a network news client
Exception	NntpProtocol Exception	signals error in return data from NNTP server
	UnknownNewsgroup Exception	signals that requested news group is not recognized

net.www.content.image

The **net.www.content.image** package contains special API functions and capabilities for the contents of WWW image objects. To include the classes of this package, use this Java code:

```
// import all items in net.www.content.image package
import net.www.content.image.*;
```

Table A-10 summarizes all the classes in the **net.www.content.image** package.

Table A-10: Classes of the net.www.content.image Package

PACKAGE ELEMENT	NAME	DESCRIPTION
Class	gif	provides retrieval of .GIF image content

Table A-10: *Continued*

PACKAGE ELEMENT	NAME	DESCRIPTION
	x_xbitmap	provides retrieval of X bitmap image content
	x_xpixmap	provides retrieval of X pixmap image content

net.www.html

The **net.www.html** class provides special API functions and capabilities for HTML documents. To include the interface, and all classes and exceptions of this package, use this Java code:

```
// import all items of the net.www.html package
import net.www.html.*;
```

Table A-11 summarizes the interface and all classes and exceptions in the **net.www.html** package.

Table A-11: Interface, Classes, and Exceptions of the net.www.html Package

PACKAGE ELEMENT	NAME	DESCRIPTION
Interface	ParserClient	??????????????
Class	ContentHandler	provides mechanisms for reading content of arbitrary MIME types
	Document	defines an HTML document
	MessageHeader	defines an MIME header
	MeteredStream	provides mechanisms to meter a data stream
	Parser	provides parsing of input stream for HTML tags
	ProgressReport	provides progress report information
	Tag	implements a set of nonstandard HTML tags
	TagRef	??????????????
	URL	implements a uniform resource

Table A-11: *Continued*

PACKAGE ELEMENT	NAME	DESCRIPTION
		locator
	URLStreamHandler	provides mechanisms to create specific protocol data streams
	WWWClassLoader	provides loading of WWW classes
Exception	FormatException	signals invalid data format
	MalformedURL Exception	signals improper URL format
	UnknownContent Exception	signals that content format is not recognized

Question marks indicate names not currently defined in the Java specification.

net.www.http

The **net.www.http** package provides special API functions and capabilities for the Hypertext Transport Protocol (HTTP) of the WWW. To include all classes and the exception of the package, use this Java code:

```
// import all items of the net.www.http package
import net.www.http.*;
```

Table A-12 summarizes the classes and the exception in the **net.www.http** package.

Table A-12: Classes and Exception of the net.www.http Package

PACKAGE ELEMENT	NAME	DESCRIPTION
Class	AuthenticationInfo	provides user authentication mechanisms
	HttpClient	implements an HTTP client
Exception	UnauthorizedHttp RequestException	signals that the HTTP client request was not authorized by the HTTP server

Java Language
Grammar

his is a short grammar for a Java compilation unit. Because a Java program consists of one or more compilation units, you can generalize from the compilation unit level to the program level for both applets and applications.

The grammar has undefined terminal symbols of DocComment, Identifier, String, and Character. Quoted text signifies literal terminals (e.g., '(' indicates the mandatory presence of a left parenthesis).

Each rule is of the form:

```
nonterminal = meta-expression ;
```

For clarity, each rule ends with a final semicolon on its own line and is separated from the next rule by a blank line.

Other meta-notation includes:

- : | for alternation (either-or, one of many, etc.)
- (...) for grouping
- postfix ? for 0 or 1 occurrences required
- postfix + for 1 or more occurrence required
- postfix * for 0 or more occurrences required

This is a BNF-like grammar, but doesn't explicitly follow Wirth's production rules. For automated parsing, some meta-symbol and punctuation must be reformatted. (BNF stands for Backus-Naur Form, a specific computer language notation developed in the 1970s that is commonly used to describe languages formally and completely; if you've ever learned Pascal or Modula 2, the chances are good that you've seen a BNF grammar.)

```
CompilationUnit =
 PackageStatement? ImportStatement* TypeDeclaration*
;


PackageStatement =
 'package' PackageName ';'
;


ImportStatement =
 'import' PackageName '.' '*' ';'
 | 'import' ( ClassName | InterfaceName )';'
;
TypeDeclaration =
   DocComment? ClassDeclaration
|  DocComment? InterfaceDeclaration
|  ';'
;


ClassDeclaration =
   Modifier* 'class' Identifier
   ('extends' ClassName)?
   ('implements' InterfaceName (',' InterfaceName)*)?
   '{' FieldDeclaration* '}'
;


InterfaceDeclaration =
   Modifier* 'interface' Identifier
   ('extends' InterfaceName (',' InterfaceName)*)?
   '{' FieldDeclaration* '}'
;
FieldDeclaration =
   DocComment? MethodDeclaration
|  DocComment? ConstructorDeclaration
|  DocComment? VariableDeclaration
```

224

```
|   StaticInitializer
|   ';'
;


MethodDeclaration =
  Modifier* Type Identifier '(' ParameterList? ')' ( '[' ']' )*
  ( '{' Statement* '}' | ';' )
;


ConstructorDeclaration =
  Modifier* Identifier '(' ParameterList? ')'
  '{' Statement* '}'
;


VariableDeclaration =
  Modifier* Type VariableDeclarator (',' VariableDeclarator)* ';'
;


VariableDeclarator =
  Identifier ('[' ']')* ('=' VariableInitializer)?
;


VariableInitializer  =
  Expression
| '{'  ( VariableInitializer  ( ',' VariableInitializer  )* ','? )? '}'
;


StaticInitializer =
  'static' '{' Statement* '}'
;
ParameterList =
  Parameter (',' Parameter)*
;
Parameter =
  Type Identifier ('[' ']')*
;

Statement =
```

```
  VariableDeclaration
|  Expression ';'
|  '{' Statement* '}'
|  'if' '(' Expression ')' Statement ('else' Statement)?
|  'while' '(' Expression ')' Statement
|  'do' Statement 'while' '(' Expression ')' ';'
|  'for' '(' ( VariableDeclaration |Expression ';' | ';')
        Expression ? ';' Expression ?')' Statement
|  'try' Statement ('catch' '(' Parameter ')' Statement)*
    ('finally' Statement)?
|  'switch' '(' Expression ')' '{'
    ( 'case' Expression ':' | 'default' ':' | Statement ) *
  '}'
|  'synchronized' ''' Expression ')' Statement
|  'return' Expression? ';'
|  'throw' Expression ';'
|  Identifier ':' Statement
|  'break' Identifier? ';'
|  'continue' Identifier? ';'
|  ';'
;


Expression =
  Expression '+' Expression
|  Expression '-' Expression
|  Expression '*' Expression
|  Expression '/' Expression
|  Expression '%' Expression
|  Expression '^' Expression
|  Expression '&' Expression
|  Expression '|' Expression
|  Expression '&&' Expression
|  Expression '||' Expression
|  Expression '<<' Expression
|  Expression '>>' Expression
|  Expression '>>>' Expression
|  Expression '=' Expression
|  Expression '+=' Expression
|  Expression '-=' Expression
```

226

```
|   Expression '*=' Expression
|   Expression '/=' Expression
|   Expression '%=' Expression
|   Expression '^=' Expression
|   Expression '&=' Expression
|   Expression '|=' Expression
|   Expression '<<=' Expression
|   Expression '>>=' Expression
|   Expression '>>>=' Expression
|   Expression '<' Expression
|   Expression '>' Expression
|   Expression '<=' Expression
|   Expression '>=' Expression
|   Expression '==' Expression
|   Expression '!=' Expression
|   Expression '.' Expression
|   Expression ',' Expression
|   Expression 'instanceof' ( ClassName | InterfaceName )
|   Expression '?' Expression ':' Expression
|   Expression '[' Expression ']'
|   '++' Expression
|   '--' Expression
|   Expression '++'
|   Expression '--'
|   '-' Expression
|   '!' Expression
|   '~' Expression
|   '(' Expression  ')'
|   '(' Type ')' Expression
|   Expression  '(' ArgList? ')'
|   'new' ClassName  '(' ArgList?')'
|   'new' TypeSpecifier  ( '[' Expression ']' )+ ('['  ']')*
|   'new' '(' Expression  ')'
|   'true'
|   'false'
|   'null'
|   'super'
|   'this'
|   Identifier
```

227

```
      |   IntegerLiteral
      |   FloatLiteral
      |   String
      |   Character
      ;


ArgList =
    Expression (',' Expression )*
  ;


Type =
    TypeSpecifier ('[' ']')*
  ;


TypeSpecifier =
     'boolean'
  |  'byte'
  |  'char'
  |  'short'
  |  'int'
  |  'float'
  |  'long'
  |  'double'
  |  ClassName
  |  InterfaceName
  ;


Modifier =
     'public'
  |  'private'
  |  'protected'
  |  'static'
  |  'final'
  |  'native'
  |  'synchronized'
  |  'abstract'
  |  'threadsafe'
  |  'transient'
  ;
```

228

```
PackageName =
  Identifier
|  PackageName '.' Identifier
;


ClassName =
  Identifier
|    PackageName '.' Identifier
;


InterfaceName =
  Identifier
|    PackageName '.' Identifier
;


IntegerLiteral =
   ('1'|...|'9')('0'|...|'9')*('L'|'l')?
|   '0'('1'|...|'7')*('L'|'l')?
|   '0'('x'|'X')('0'|...|'9'|'a'|...|'f'|'A'|...|'F')+('L'|'l')?
;


FloatLiteral =
   DecimalDigits '.' DecimalDigits? ExponentPart? FloatTypeSuffix?
|   '.'DecimalDigits ExponentPart? FloatTypeSuffix?
|   DecimalDigits ExponentPart FloatTypeSuffix?
;


DecimalDigits =
  ('0'|...|'9')+
;


ExponentPart =
  ( 'E' | 'e' )( '+' | '-' )? DecimalDigits
;


FloatTypeSuffix =
    'F' | 'f' | 'D' | 'd'
;
```

Glossary

.gif (also .GIF; Graphics Interchange Format). A compressed graphics file format patented by Unisys and widely used in HTML documents for in-line graphical elements.

.tar. An abbreviation for tape archive, *tar* is the eponymous UNIX command that groups related individual files into .tar-format files. *Untar* is the operation of removing the original files from the parent *tar*red file, even though you use the command *tar -xvf junk.tar* to decompose the file named junk.tar.

.Z. A file format associated with the UNIX *compress* program. Use the UNIX *uncompress* or gzip program to decompress .Z-format files.

abstract. A brief restatement of the contents of a file or document; or, when applied to Java classes, an uninstantiable class that defines runtime behavior rather than objects.

algorithm. A step-by-step, programmatic recipe for producing a certain set of results in a computer program.

alias. A computer system name that points at another name instead of at an underlying object. Most Web URLs are either wholly or partly aliases to protect the underlying file system on the Web server to which they point.

alpha. A way of rating the completion status of a piece of software, alpha indicates that it's still in internal testing and generally has not yet been released outside its development organization.

anchor. An HTML term for the destination end of a link; it may some-times be used as a synonym for hypertext links of all kinds.

animation. The use of computer graphics to prepare moving sequences of images; or, any graphic method that creates the illusion of motion by rapid viewing of individual frames in sequence.

ANSI (American National Standards Institute). One of the primary stan-dards-setting bodies for computer technology in the United States.

API (Application Programming Interface). Usually, a set of interface subroutines or library calls that define the methods for programs to access external services (i.e., to somebody else's system or program).

application independence. A format or facility is application inde-pendent when it works in multiple environments and doesn't depend on a specific application to understand or use its contents.

architecture. The design of a software or hardware system as a con-nected set of logical building blocks with sufficient detail to allow each block to be completely designed and implemented, and to allow blocks that interact to successfully communicate with one another.

argument. A positional placeholder for a specific type of value to be passed into a function, method, or constructor to establish the value of a mapping, or the results of an operation.

ASCII (American Standard Code for Information Interchange). A stan-dard encoding for text and control characters in binary format that is widely used on most computers.

asynchronous. Literally "not at the same time," the term refers to com-puter communication in which sender and receiver do not communi-cate directly with one another, but rather through accessing a common pick-up/drop-off point for information.

attribute. In most object-oriented programming languages, including Java, an attribute is a named component of an object or term with spe-cific value typing, element definitions, requirements, and defaults.

authentication. A method for identifying a user prior to granting per-mission to access, change, or delete a system or network resource. It usually depends on a password.

back end. Computer science jargon for a service that runs on a machine elsewhere on the network, usually driven by an interface or query facility from another machine elsewhere on the network (the front end).

behavior. A programmatic way of establishing how an object acts, behavior describes characteristics that determine responses or actions when impinged upon by other objects.

beta. Beta indicates the status of software under development that has been released outside its development organization to a select group of recipients for testing or evaluation purposes prior to commercial release.

binary. Literally, this means that a file is formatted as a collection of ones and zeros; in practice, it means that a file is formatted to be intelligible only to a certain application, or that it is itself an executable file.

binary executables. Files created by compiling and linking source code modules so they can be executed or run by computer users.

BIND (Berkeley Internet Name Domain). BIND is the most popular implementation of the Internet Domain Name Service in use today. Written by Kevin Dunlap for 4.3BSD UNIX, BIND supplies a distributed database capability that lets multiple DNS servers cooperate to resolve Internet names into correct IP addresses.

bitmap. A two-dimensional map of binary digits (bits) destined for use in a one-to-one mapping with a display device's pixels to produce a graphic image.

boot. Often used in computer-speak as a verb, boot means to start a computer from its turned-off state.

bottleneck. A point in a computer or a network at which events become congested and slow down.

boundary errors. In programming, errors can occur within the range of the expected data, outside that range, or right on the edges of the expected range. When errors occur at the edges, they're called boundary errors—e.g., if a number between 1 and 100 is acceptable, what happens with 1 or 100?

breakpoint. A marked location in a program, usually set with a debugger or an equivalent tool, where the program halts execution so the programmer can examine values such as variables, parameters, and settings.

browser. An Internet application that lets users access WWW servers and surf the Net. HotJava is currently the only browser that supports Java applets embedded in HTML documents.

BSDI (Berkeley Software Distribution, Inc.). BSDI remains a major flavor of UNIX today.

bug. Programmer-speak for an error, glitch, gotcha, problem, or unsolved mystery in a computer program.

bytecode. The platform-independent intermediate format created by the Java compiler from source code used by the runtime environment to execute the corresponding Java applet or application.

C. A programming language developed by two of the founders of UNIX, Brian Kernighan and Dennis Ritchie, still very much in vogue among UNIX-heads.

C++. A programming language developed by Bjarne Stroustrup, C++ is an object-oriented extension of, and successor to, the C language.

case sensitive. This means that upper- and lowercase letters are not equivalent. (For example, UNIX filenames are case sensitive; TEXT.TXT is not the equivalent of text.txt.)

CD-ROM (Compact Disk–Read–Only Memory). A read–only computer medium that looks like a music compact disk, but contains computer data instead of music.

CGI (Common Gateway Interface). The parameter passing and invocation technique that lets Web clients pass input to Web servers and on to specific programs written to the CGI specification.

child. In general OO terminology, a child is an object that inherits from and specializes another object; in Java, this means a child class inherits from another class, called a parent or superclass.

class. An object-oriented programming term, class refers to a method for defining a set of related objects that can inherit or share certain characteristics.

clickable image. A graphic in an HTML document that has been associated to a pixel-mapping CGI on the server; users click locations on the graphic to retrieve its associated URL.

client pull. A method through which a Web client can instruct a server to send it a particular set of data. Java applets provide this functionality to properly-equipped browsers as a matter of course.

client/server. A computing paradigm wherein processing is divided between a front-end application running on a user's desktop machine and a back-end server that performs tasks in response to client service requests.

client. Used as (a) a synonym for Web browser (i.e., Web client), or (b) a requesting, front-end member for client-server applications.

close. A formal communication term that refers to session tear down and termination, usually at the end of a networked information transaction.

compiler. A software program that reads the source code for a programming language and creates a binary executable version of that code. The Java compiler creates a platform-independent intermediary format instead, called a bytecode, so the same Java code can be interpreted on a variety of platforms.

compliant. Conforms to a defined standard of some kind.

connection. A link opened between two computers for communication.

constructor. A special method that initializes a type, called at the point of definition or when using the *new* operator.

content. The hard, usable information contained in a document. Users surf the Web looking for content.

Content-Type. The MIME designation for file types to be transported by electronic mail and HTTP.

data content model. SGML-speak for the occurrence notation that describes what other markup is legal within the context of a specific markup element.

DBMS (database management system). A set of programs and utilities that define, maintain, and manage access to collections of data, such as on-line data.

debugger. A programming tool used to control the execution of programs so they can be halted and queried.

declaration. Introduces one or many names for an object, function, type, method, etc., into a program without specifying the implementation of methods. A declaration tells a compiler that data or functions exist and supplies their names, but does not indicate where or how they're used.

definition. A definition supplies the body for a named (declared) object; it consists of a collection of statements enclosed in braces ({}) in Java, which indicate the beginning and end of a block of code.

delimiter. A designated text character that indicates a record or field boundary within a text stream rather than being interpreted as a part of the text itself.

destructor. A special type of method that performs cleanup for a user-defined object type and reclaims its allocated memory and, when applicable, other resources.

development environment. The collection of tools, compilers, debuggers, and source code management resources used as part of the software development process.

directory structure. The hierarchical organization of files in a directory tree.

DNS (Domain Name Service). An Internet service that maps symbolic names to IP addresses by distributing queries among the available pool of DNS servers. (See Bind.)

document annotation. The process of attaching comments, instructions, or additional information to a document (usually with annotation software for electronic copy).

document root. The base of a Web server's document tree, the root defines the scope of all the documents that Web users may access (i.e., access is allowed to the root and its children, but not to the root's peers or parents).

document tree. A description of all directories and documents underneath the document's root.

e-mail (electronic mail). A service that lets users exchange messages across a network; the major e-mail technology in use on the Internet is based on SMTP (Simple Mail Transfer Protocol).

editor. A program used to edit a file; editors for specific programming languages, markup languages, and text formats are available.

element. A basic unit of text or markup within a descriptive markup language.

element type. The kind of value that an element can take, such as text, number, or tag.

encapsulation. Combining data with the methods used for its manipulation; e.g., organizing code into user-defined types.

encoding. A technique for expressing values according to a particular type of notation, such as binary, ASCII, or EBCDIC.

environment variables. Like other UNIX programs, CGIs obtain and store their input rather than reading it every time it's needed. This stored information—in the form of environment variables—is passed to the program by the HTTP server from the submitting client. An environment variable, therefore, is a value passed into a program or script by the runtime environment on the system on which it's running.

error checking. The process of examining input data to make sure it is both appropriate (within specified value or scalar ranges) and accurate (correctly reflects the input).

event. An occurrence from the world outside a program that affects its behavior (e.g., arrival of a message, keystroke, mouse click, or system occurrence).

exception handling. If a program behaves abnormally, encounters an unexpected input, or detects an anomaly in its operation, it must react. This is called exception handling.

extensibility. A measure of how easy it is to write applications that build upon core mechanisms while adding functionality, new methods, or subclasses.

extension language. A programming language, like Python, that can extend the functionality of programmable languages or interfaces.

FAQs (frequently asked questions). A list of common questions with their answers maintained by most special interest groups on the Internet to lower the frequency of directly responding to basic technical questions.

field. In a database, a named component of a record and its associated values; in an HTML form, a named input widget or text area and its associated value.

file mapping. A method of supplying a filename to the outside world that does not reveal the complete internal file structures involved. (See also **alias**.)

filtering. The process of removing certain objects from a document. For example, removing processing instructions important to a specific scheme not used in a general markup scheme eliminates unintelligible material.

front end. The user interface side of a client-server application, the front end is what users see and interact with.

ftp (file transfer protocol). An Internet protocol and service that provides network file transfer between two network nodes for which a user has file access rights (often between a remote host and your local host or desktop machine).

GUI (graphical user interface). A generic name for any computer interface that uses graphics, windows, icons, and a pointing device instead of a purely character-mode interface. Microsoft Windows, MacOS, and X11 are examples of GUIs.

helper applications. Applications invoked outside a Web browser to render, display, or play data that the browser itself cannot handle, such as multimedia files.

hierarchical. A form of document or file structure, also known as a tree structure, in which all elements except the root have parents, and all elements may or may not have children.

HTML (HyperText Markup Language). The text-based descriptive hypertext markup language derived from SGML used to describe documents for the WWW.

HTTP (HyperText Transfer Protocol). The TCP/IP-based communication protocol developed for the WWW, HTTP defines how Web clients and servers communicate.

httpd (HTTP daemon). The daemon or listener program on a Web server that responds to requests for Web documents or CGI-based services.

hypermedia. Any method of nonlinear, computer-based information delivery, including text, graphics, video, animation, and sound, that can be interlinked and treated as a single collection of information.

hypertext. A method of organizing text for computer use that lets individual data elements point to one another; a nonlinear method of organizing textual information.

inheritance. The OO term that indicates that objects subordinate to parent objects or classes obtain attributes, properties, or behaviors from superordinate objects. The objects inherit these elements from elements higher in the object hierarchy.

initialization. To set a variable or an instance of a type to a specific value, usually at start-up or upon instantiation.

instance. A particular incarnation of an object, class, or record, an instance includes the data for a single, specific item in a data collection.

instantiate. A runtime operation that creates a particular incarnation of an object, class, or record that contains data about a single, specific item in a data collection.

interface. The particular subroutines, parameter-passing mechanisms, and data that define the way two systems (which may be on the same or different machines) communicate with one another. For Java, this corresponds to the class declaration, which describes what a type does. The implementation describes how the type works.

international standard. In many areas of technology, standards among countries are established, controlled, or honored by the International Standards Organization (ISO).

Internet. The worldwide, TCP/IP-based computing network with millions of users that links government, business, research, industry, individuals, and education.

interpreter. A software program that reads and interprets the instructions contained within source code from a programming language every time it is run. The alternative is a compiler, which translates source code into a binary form only once, which is then executed instead. Java takes the middle road, using a compiler to create an intermediate format, called bytecode, that is then interpreted by the Java runtime system.

IP (Internet Protocol). The primary network layer protocol for the TCP/IP protocol suite, IP is probably the most widely-used network protocol in the world.

ISP (Internet Service Provider). Any organization that provides Internet access to a consumer, usually for a fee.

jpeg (also JPEG; Joint Photographic Experts Group). A highly-compressible graphics format designed to handle computer images of high-resolution photographs efficiently.

keyword. An essential or definitive term used to index data for later search and retrieval; in programming languages, this term sometimes describes a word that is part of the language itself. (See also reserved word.)

kludge. A programming term for a workaround or an inelegant solution to a problem.

LAN (local area network). A network linked by physical cables or short-haul connections across a span of generally less than one mile.

library. A collection of programs or code modules that programmers link to their own code to provide standard, predefined functionality.

link. A basic element of hypertext, a link provides a method for jumping from one point in a document to another point in the same document, or to another document altogether.

MacOS. An abbreviation for Macintosh Operating System.

mail server. Any member of a class of Internet programs (e.g., *majordomo, listserv,* or *mailserv*) that allows users to participate in ongoing data exchanges or file retrieval via electronic mail.

mailing list. The list of participants who exchange electronic mail messages regularly, usually focused on a particular topic or concern.

map files. The boundary definitions for a clickable image, stored in a file format for a particular HTTP server implementation (usually NCSA or CERN), used to assign URLs to regions on an image for user navigation.

markup. A special form of text embedded in a document that describes elements of document structure, layout, presentation, or delivery.

message. The name of a method passed to an instance of an object type; when you send a message to an object instance, that results in calling one of its methods using dot notation as in **Object.method( );**.

metalanguage. A formal language like SGML that is used to describe other languages.

method. A function declared within a class used to access data within that class. (In C++, this is also called a member function.)

MIME (Multipurpose Internet Mail Extensions). Extensions to the RFC822 mail message format to permit more complex data and file types than plain text. Today, MIME types include sound, video, graphics, PostScript, and HTML.

modularity. The concept that a program should be broken into components, each of which supplies a particular function or capability.

Motif. A UNIX-based GUI.

multithreaded. A characteristic of a computer runtime environment that uses a lightweight process control mechanism, called *threading*, to switch contexts among multiple tasks.

net-pointers. URLs, FTP addresses, or other locations on the Internet where you can go to get the good stuff.

network services. Access to shared files, printers, data, or other applications (e.g., e-mail or scheduling) across a network.

network utilization. The amount of network usage, usually expressed as the percentage of bandwidth consumed on the medium, for a specific period of time.

newsgroup. On USENET, an individual topic area is called a *newsgroup*. Individuals who use such areas exchange regular message traffic and can be a great source of information for technical topics of all kinds.

NULL. In programming and in more general computing terms, NULL is a representation for a missing or empty value.

object oriented. A programming paradigm that concentrates on defining data objects and the methods that may be applied to them.

OO. OO is the abbreviation for object oriented.

package. In Java, a package is the compilation unit that sets scoping boundaries for the **private** keyword (i.e., meaning that a variable, object, etc. is only defined within the scope of the package that declares it as **private**). Packages contain declarations and implementations that are treated as a single run-time execution unit.

parameter. A value passed into or out of a program or subroutine, or across an interface, when code components communicate with one another.

parent. An OO term that indicates that one object is a generalization or an ancestor of another by inheritance.

parse tree. A graphical representation of the designation of, and relationships between, tokens or lexical elements in an input stream that has been parsed.

pattern matching. A computerized search operation whereby input values are treated as patterns and matches are sought in a search database. An exact match is called a *hit*; the results of a search produce a list of hits for further investigation.

pixel (picture element). A single, addressable location on a computer display, a pixel is the most primitive element for controlling graphics. A pixel is also the term for how image maps are measured and specified.

placeholder. A symbolic representation of a value that will be manipulated by a program, but only when it's running and an initial input value is defined. While code is being written, all parameters are merely placeholders.

platform independent. This characteristic indicates that a program or device runs on any computer.

port address. In TCP/IP-speak, a port address refers to the socket identifier that a program or a service seeks to address for a specific type of communication. Most TCP/IP protocols have well-known port addresses associated with them (e.g., HTTP's port address is 80). But system configurations allow other port addresses, which can be a good idea for security.

port (short for transport, usually used as a verb). In computer jargon, porting code refers to altering a program written for one system so it runs on another system.

PostScript. A page description language defined by Adobe Systems and the files written in that language. PostScript files usually carry a .ps extension in the UNIX world and are a common file structure for exchanging formatted print files.

private. Instances following the **private** keyword can be accessed only by methods declared within the same class.

protected. Instances following the keyword **protected** can only be accessed by methods within the same class or methods within classes derived from that class (i.e., for which that class is their superclass).

public. Java objects, variables, etc., declared with the keyword **public** are available to an entire program irrespective of package boundaries.

processor intensive. An application that consumes lots of CPU cycles is said to be processor intensive. Good examples include heavy graphics rendering such as ray-tracing, animation, CAD, and other programs that combine lots of number crunching with intensive display requirements.

properties. The values of an object's attributes, or the significance of the attributes themselves, endow an object with properties that distinguish it from other objects.

proprietary. Technology that's owned or controlled by a company or organization.

protocol suite. A collection of networking protocols that together define a complete set of tools and communication facilities for network access and use (e.g., TCP/IP, OSI, or IPX/SPX).

query string. The parameters passed to a search engine, usually using the GET method in the case of Web-based searches.

remote location. A site or machine elsewhere on a network, remote location can also refer to a machine that is only intermittently connected to a network.

render. To interpret the contents of a document, image, or other file so that it can be displayed or played back on a computer.

repository. A place where data are kept, like a file archive, database server, or document management system.

request. A network message from a client to a server that states the need for a particular item of information or a service.

request header. The preamble to a request, the header identifies the requester and provides authentication and formatting information where applicable. This lets the server know where to send a response, whether or not that request should be honored, and what formats it may take.

reserved word. A word in the Java language set aside for special use only; i.e., you cannot use <BOLD>sqrt</BOLD> as a variable name.

.response. A network message from a server to a client that contains a reply to a request for service.

response header. The preamble to a response, the header identifies the sender and the application to which the response should be supplied.

response time. The amount of time that elapses between the transmission of a request for service and the arrival of the corresponding response.

reusability. The degree to which programs, modules, or subroutines have been designed and implemented for multifunction use. The easier it is to employ the same code in a number of applications, the greater is that code's degree of reusability.

runtime variables. Program input or output values that cannot be assigned until the program is running.

runtime system. For Java, this is the execution environment that interprets bytecodes, checks their integrity and security, and applies dynamic (runtime) bindings based on current system states, environment variables, and input parameters.

search string. The input passed for keyword search and pattern matching in an index to a search engine or database management system.

server push. A Netscape-designed technique to let a server initiate data transfer, especially useful for time-sensitive data like voice or video, for which rapid delivery is crucial for continuity and intelligibility. Available as a matter of course from Java applets and applications.

server. A computer that provides services to other computers via a network.

Standard Generalized Markup Language (SGML). An ISO standard (ISO-8879) document definition, specification, and creation metalanguage that makes platform and display differences across multiple computers irrelevant to the delivery and rendering of documents. SGML is entirely suitable for describing all kinds of markup languages, and in fact was used to describe HTML.

signal-to-noise ratio. In Web-speak, the ratio of good information to junk in a newsgroup or mailing list.

source code. The text files containing instructions in a particular programming language that programmers write when creating software.

specification. A document that describes the requirements, inputs and outputs, and capabilities of a protocol, service, language, or software program (a kind of blueprint for a computer system or service of some kind).

standard. A program, system, protocol, or other computer component that has been declared a standard may be the result of an official standards-setting body or it may simply have acquired that status through widespread or long-term use. When talking about standards, it's important to determine whether the designation is official.

standards aware. Describes software that understands standards and works within their constraints.

standards compliant. Describes software that rigorously implements all of a standard's requirements and capabilities.

static. An instance of an object allocated in the data segment and on the stack; in Java, static instances have global lifetimes, are initialized before execution begins, and are cleaned up after it ends.

static method. A method resolved at compile time through early binding as opposed to runtime binding.

step-by-step execution. When debugging a program, locating the exact line of code where an error occurs can be essential to detecting and fixing the problem. Debuggers let developers *step through* their code for this reason.

stepwise refinement. A phrase coined by Edsger Dijkstra to indicate the repeated respecification and analysis of program elements needed to create elegant designs and implementations.

string. In programmer-speak, a string consists of character data like "Mark" or "Ed too."

symbolic link. A mechanism whereby one name points to another name in a system rather than directly to an object. Symbolic names are common for Web servers, document roots, and other system objects.

synchronous. A method of communications wherein all communicating parties send and receive data in the same order.

syntax. The rules for placing and ordering terms, punctuation, and values when writing statements in a particular language—including programming languages, in which the rules tend to be rather exacting.

system administrator. The individual responsible for maintaining a computer system, managing the network, setting up accounts, installing applications, etc.

tar (tape archive). A UNIX utility that archives related files into a single file. (See also **.tar**.)

Tcl (Tool command language, pronounced "tickle"). Tcl is a simple scripting language for extending and controlling applications. Tcl can be embedded into C applications because its interpreter is implemented as a C library of procedures. Each application can extend the basic Tcl functions by creating new Tcl commands that are specific to a particular programming task.

TCP/IP (Transmission Control Protocol/Internet Protocol). The basic suite of protocols upon which the Internet runs.

telnet. A TCP/IP protocol and service that lets a user on one computer communicate with another computer and emulate a terminal attached to it.

template. An example or pattern for a program or document that acts as a predefined skeleton that must be filled in.

toolset. A collection of software tools useful for performing certain tasks (e.g., CGI input handling or image map creation).

tree. A hierarchical structure for organizing data or documents, common examples of which include file system directories, object hierarchies, and family trees.

type. Indicates the range of values or states that a variable can assume and, consequently, indicates the operators that can be applied.

type extensibility. The ability to add functionality to code by deriving new types through inheritance (X extends Y, in Java parlance), to add or modify behaviors to suit specific application or implementation needs.

UNIX. The powerful operating system developed by Brian Kernighan and Dennis Ritchie as a form of recreation at Bell Labs in the late 1960s and still running strong today.

URI (Uniform Resource Identifier). Any of a class of objects that identify resources available to the Web; both URLs and URNs are instances of URIs.

URL (Uniform Resource Locator). The primary naming scheme that identifies Web resources, URLs define the protocols to be used, the domain name of the Web server where a resource resides, the port address for communication, and the directory path to access a Web document or resource.

URL encoding. A method for passing information requests and URL specifications to Web servers from browsers, URL encoding replaces spaces with plus signs and substitutes hex codes for a range of otherwise irreproducible characters. This method is used to pass document queries (via the GET method) from browser to server, and on to CGIs.

URN (Uniform Resource Name). A permanent, unchanging name for a Web resource; seldom used in today's Web environment.

USENET. An Internet protocol and service that provides access to a vast array of named *newsgroups*, where users congregate to exchange information and materials related to specific topics.

USENET hierarchy. The way in which newsgroups are organized is hierarchical. The most interesting collection of newsgroups from the standpoint of this book is the *comp.infosystems.www* hierarchy.

vector. A line segment described by two vertices, or location coordinates in a Cartesian space, used to display that line.

version control. An important aspect of a source code or document management system, version control refers to the ability to associate particular versions of documents or programs. This may be necessary to maintain a production version and a development version for a program.

Web. (See **World Wide Web**.)

Web sites. Individual Web document collections named by home pages or other unique URLs.

Webification. The act of turning electronic documents in some other format into HTML, usually programmatically rather than by hand.

Webify. The verb form of Webification; see preceding definition.

WebMaster. The individual responsible for managing a specific Web site.

Web space. The total agglomeration of sites, resources, and documents available through the World Wide Web.

World Wide Web. The total information space and services provided by all the Web servers available through the Internet. Tim Berners-Lee, one of the Web's primary designers and implementers, referred to the Web as "the embodiment of human knowledge" in his seminal definition paper on the subject. For some interesting information on how it all began, please consult:

http://www.cern.ch/CERN/WorldWideWeb/Intro/start.html.

WWW. (See World Wide Web.)

X11. The GUI standard that governs X Windows, controlled by the X/Open Corporation (also the owner of the UNIX trademark and design).

X Windows. A windowed graphical user interface governed by X11 that's widely used in the UNIX community.

Yahoo (Yet Another Hierarchical Officious Oracle). Yahoo is a database written and maintained by David Filo and Jerry Yang, who style themselves "self-proclaimed Yahoos." This is an inauspicious introduction to one of the best search engines for the World Wide Web. When we go surfing, we often start from Yahoo!

Index

IDG BOOKS

Order Center: **(800) 762-2974** *(8 a.m.–6 p.m., EST, weekdays)*

5/8/95

Quantity	ISBN	Title	Price	Total

Shipping & Handling Charges

	Description	First book	Each additional book	Total
Domestic	Normal	$4.50	$1.50	$
	Two Day Air	$8.50	$2.50	$
	Overnight	$18.00	$3.00	$
International	Surface	$8.00	$8.00	$
	Airmail	$16.00	$16.00	$
	DHL Air	$17.00	$17.00	$

*For large quantities call for shipping & handling charges.
**Prices are subject to change without notice.

Ship to:

Name _____

Company _____

Address _____

City/State/Zip _____

Daytime Phone _____

Payment: ☐ Check to IDG Books (US Funds Only)

☐ VISA   ☐ MasterCard   ☐ American Express

Card # _____ Expires _____

Signature _____

Subtotal _____

CA residents add
applicable sales tax _____

IN, MA, and MD
residents add
5% sales tax _____

IL residents add
6.25% sales tax _____

RI residents add
7% sales tax _____

TX residents add
8.25% sales tax _____

Shipping _____

Total _____

Please send this order form to:

**IDG Books Worldwide
7260 Shadeland Station, Suite 100
Indianapolis, IN 46256**

*Allow up to 3 weeks for delivery.
Thank you!*

IDG BOOKS WORLDWIDE REGISTRATION CARD

RETURN THIS REGISTRATION CARD FOR FREE CATALOG

Title of this book: The Internet World 60 Minute Guide To Java

My overall rating of this book: ❑ Very good [1]   ❑ Good [2]   ❑ Satisfactory [3]   ❑ Fair [4]   ❑ Poor [5]

How I first heard about this book:

❑ Found in bookstore; name: [6]

❑ Advertisement: [8]

❑ Word of mouth; heard about book from friend, co-worker, etc.: [10]

❑ Book review: [7]

❑ Catalog: [9]

❑ Other: [11]

What I liked most about this book:

What I would change, add, delete, etc., in future editions of this book:

Other comments:

Number of computer books I purchase in a year: ❑ 1 [12]   ❑ 2-5 [13]   ❑ 6-10 [14]   ❑ More than 10 [15]

I would characterize my computer skills as: ❑ Beginner [16] ❑ Intermediate [17] ❑ Advanced [18] ❑ Professional [19]

I use ❑ DOS [20] ❑ Windows [21] ❑ OS/2 [22] ❑ Unix [23] ❑ Macintosh [24] ❑ Other: [25]_____
(please specify)

I would be interested in new books on the following subjects:
(please check all that apply, and use the spaces provided to identify specific software)

❑ Word processing: [26]

❑ Data bases: [28]

❑ File Utilities: [30]

❑ Networking: [32]

❑ Other: [34]

❑ Spreadsheets: [27]

❑ Desktop publishing: [29]

❑ Money management: [31]

❑ Programming languages: [33]

I use a PC at (please check all that apply): ❑ home [35]   ❑ work [36]   ❑ school [37]   ❑ other: [38] _____

The disks I prefer to use are ❑ 5.25 [39] ❑ 3.5 [40] ❑ other: [41]_____

I have a CD ROM: ❑ yes [42]   ❑ no [43]

I plan to buy or upgrade computer hardware this year: ❑ yes [44]   ❑ no [45]

I plan to buy or upgrade computer software this year: ❑ yes [46]   ❑ no [47]

Name: Business title: [48]   Type of Business: [49]

Address (❑ home [50] ❑ work [51]/Company name: _____)

Street/Suite#

City [52]/State [53]/Zipcode [54]:   Country [55]

❑ **I liked this book!** You may quote me by name in future
IDG Books Worldwide promotional materials.

My daytime phone number is _____

IDG BOOKS

THE WORLD OF
COMPUTER
KNOWLEDGE

 # YES!
Please keep me informed about IDG's World of Computer Knowledge.
Send me the latest IDG Books catalog.

COMPUTER
BOOK SERIES
FROM IDG